GROWING DISCIPLES THROUGH PREACHING

Growing Disciples Through Preaching

NOLAN P. HOWINGTON
ALTON H. McEACHERN
WILLIAM M. PINSON, JR.

Broadman Press/Nashville, Tennessee

4222-27
ISBN: 0-8054-2227-7

Dewey Decimal Classification: 248.4
Subject headings: CHRISTIAN LIFE // SERMONS

Library of Congress Catalog Card Number: 75-41741
Printed in the United States of America

Introduction

The pastor of a large suburban church has concluded that building disciples must become a major part of his work—if he is to get his work done! This conclusion was born of frustration in the face of heavy pastoral duties. It also grew out of an awareness that equipping church members for the work of ministry (Eph. 4:12) is at the heart of pastoral responsibility, as well as the biblical way to build up the church.

"Disciple" and "discipleship" are terms that suggest learning, training, motivation, and inspiration. These are the ingredients that meet us in the gospel accounts where the Master Teacher is training his followers. Admittedly, intensive training best occurs in small groups. What, then, is the function of Christian preaching in the process of building discipleship?

There is a kind of preaching that sifts the hearts of persons and may even turn some away (John 6:60,66). Authentic gospel preaching always keeps the full demands of Christian discipleship before people. Cheap, sensational stunts and shallow, entertaining sermons may attract crowds—but so does a carnival. But these do not bring individuals to genuine commitment to the person of Jesus Christ or to a life of growth and ministry in his name.

Biblical preaching comes to grips with the problems of man's sin and estrangement from God. But it also deals solidly and recurringly with God's claim upon our lives as his people. No one disputes the fact that our proclamation aims at introducing persons to Jesus Christ. But must it not, in good Pauline fashion (Rom. 10:9-13), proclaim Christ as Savior *and* Lord?

The messages in this book seek to interpret Christian discipleship in the light of the New Testament and in terms of our responsibility as Christ's followers within this present age. They make no pretence to an exhaustive treatment of Christian discipleship. Surely they will stimulate thinking and enrich the pastor's preaching as he guides his people toward growth in discipleship.

T. W. Manson once noted that Jesus called his followers to be apprentices, not mere learners. They needed learning and they got it. But Jesus' desire was that they become apprentices in Kingdom work.[1] Preaching keeps this truth alive and, when done effectively, contributes to the growth of Christians toward that high purpose.

1. T. W. Manson, *The Teaching of Jesus* (Cambridge: University Press, 1963), pp. 239-40.

Contents

PART I

Exploring Discipleship

Part 1

Exploring Discipleship

1
Life Under the Cross

Luke 9:23-26,14:28; Matt. 10:24-25,38-39; Mark 8:34-38

The title of this sermon sounds forbidding. Is life under the cross a form of servitude like "life behind the iron curtain"? Jesus' invitation to discipleship came to a subject people living under the Roman standard. His demands seemed more exacting than those of Caesar for they included suffering, rejection, even death.

But the disciple is not above his Master. Indeed, to be at all like his Master he will encounter sharp hostility and malicious opposition (Matt. 10:24-25). This is no more welcome to contemporary man than it was to Jesus' hearers in first-century Palestine. Is this why we shift the focus to *his* cross, hoping to divert attention from our own? No one in his right mind would deny the centrality of Jesus' cross in the New Testament or the life of the church. As the late scholarly English bishop, Hensley Henson, said, "Jesus Christ and him crucified" constitutes a most "satisfying summary" of our personal faith. In his cross we glory and by his cross we live.

Nonetheless, no emphasis on Jesus' cross should lead us to ignore our own. For he interpreted discipleship in terms of crossbearing. Accordingly, we must take seriously his radical demands. They will not go away. They remain to haunt us for they challenge

11

our tepid, anemic kind of harmless Christianity.

For one thing *the cross is more of a discipline than a doctrine.* Jesus summons us to bear it, to enter into a lifetime of commitment and obedience. We may argue doctrine; we must live the discipline. Nor does Jesus envision a small group of hardy souls who form an elite corps. The cross of which he speaks belongs on every believer's back. His followers may be drawn from diverse classes and races. They may bring with them a variety of gifts and personality traits. But upon each person is laid the demand of discipleship, the bearing of a cross.

Crossbearing is not the same as *cross-wearing!* Jesus probably would not object to artistic or ornamental uses of the cross. The cross as symbol may be seen on the garments we wear or the autos we drive. Once I saw a decorative cross on a chain about a shapely ankle! *Cross-wearing,* however, is not the same as crossbearing.

The symbol of the cross may properly be cut into church architecture or displayed above a baptistry or atop a steeple. It is a more fitting emblem than a weathervane, though the latter may reflect more accurately the mind of the congregation than does a cross!

Crossbearing is certainly more than a stoic endurance of our aches, pains, and frustrations! Who has not heard these words from a chronic sufferer or a disappointed person: "I guess this is my cross and I must bear it." Don't you believe it! Did you ever hear a robust, prosperous Christian talk about carrying a cross? Let us be clear in our minds about Jesus' teaching. When he calls us to take up the cross and follow him, he knows that such might include pain, deprivation, and even death. But he never meant that crossbearing was restricted to arthritis, financial losses, or social disgrace in a family! A fluctuating stock market may cross us up, but it is not our cross.

What, then, did Jesus mean? Probably we can better understand *our* cross if we seek to understand *his*. Here we are limited because he gave no definitions or detailed explanations. F. W. Dillistone once wrote, "Even Jesus, that great teacher, could not *teach* the meaning of the cross; he had to *take it up*." [1] As we best declare love by deeds, not words, so his cross in its deeper meaning is *seen* and *grasped* through the deed itself.

Jesus' cross meant first of all *an unqualified surrender of his whole being to the will of God.* Long before he bore the cross to Calvary he carried it within his heart. "I do always those things that are pleasing to him." His Gethsemane prayer of submission, "not my will but thine be done," was but an expression of his total commitment to God's claim upon his life.

Dr. Ellis Fuller once described the cross as "an achieving tool." [2] With it Jesus wrought salvation for all men. *It is the epitome of a life bent on carrying out a divine mission.* Thus Jesus on his cross is the final revelation of God's glory. One day you, the sinner, and God, the sinless, met in the broken heart of the self-sacrificing Christ. You were reconciled to God through the blood of the cross! And being truly reconciled to God, you became the light of the world, the salt of the earth. Life under the cross means a commitment to the doing of God's will. This is no short-term commitment. Crossbearing involves steadiness and constancy. Discipleship is for life. "No one who puts his hand to the plow and looks back is fit for the kingdom of God" (Luke 9:62, RSV).

In his own cross, Jesus got under the world's load of sin and misery. He sought to lift that lost world up to God. And he brought God's love down to men! To share his heart means to share his mission to a desperate humanity. His love was no mawkish senti-mentality. *It was self-giving, suffering, sacrificial, and redemptive.* He sought to help men become what God intended for them to become. Does this not indicate what your cross and mine must be? Obviously, his cross was unique. His death accomplished a special purpose, namely, God's will to save men. We can never duplicate that cross. We can only share it. Yet it some sense our cross takes on a color like his own.

W. M. Clow, the Scottish theologian and preacher, has helped us with his distinction between a *thorn, a burden, and a cross.*[3] A thorn, he says, may be some bodily ill that persists—as in Paul's case. A burden may be a load imposed on us from without, as in the case of a wife who has lost a husband or an individual left with the care of an invalid parent. A cross is a load taken up voluntarily in behalf of another, borne in Christ's name. It may involve a burden or have a thorny aspect. But it is done for others out of love, with a redemptive purpose.

Perhaps by now we begin to see what it means to be cross-bearers. *It means obedience to God's will regardless of the cost to ourselves.* This is more than a comfortable doctrine for discussion amid the air-conditioned ease of the sanctuary! It is a life of discipline lived out here on earth and it involves doing the will of God whatever the risks may be. The disciple's career may begin in an act of unconditional surrender, running up a white flag in acknowledgment of a new Master. But from the moment of surrender we are thrust into a conflict on Christ's side, obedient to his commands.

Luke notes the consistency that Christ expects of us: "Let him deny himself, and take up his cross daily and follow me" (9:23, RSV). Day in and day out, moment by moment we live out our commitment as his followers. Once we put our hand to the plow there is to be no looking back or turning away (Luke 9:62). Small wonder that Dietrich Bonhoeffer once declared that the call to follow Christ is a call to die, to die to self, to lose one's life for Christ and for others.[4] Such must be the nature of our commitment.

Jesus thus put the emphasis on performance, not mere profession. He does not disallow doctrine or personal belief. But he puts the heavy stress on living out our faith. "Why do you call me 'Lord, Lord,' and do not do what I tell you?" (Luke 6:46, RSV). Those who come to him and hear his words are expected to do them (6:47; cf. Jas. 1:22,27). Practice must flow out of profession. Creeds must be translated into deeds or the world will scoff at our religious pretenses.

A cynical soul once chided a deacon: "Yeah, I swear a little and you pray a little. But neither of us means anything by it, do we?" Jesus reserved a stern warning for men who were like tasteless, worthless salt. Is there anything in the world so useless as salt that has lost its saltiness? Life becomes flat for the person who is supposed to be the salt of the earth but has lost that quality so needed in society. Everybody loses when Christians become *nothing*.

Jesus probably knew that some sinners show more zest, vigor, and ingenuity than many of the saints (Luke 16:8). Once Gert Behenna told an audience of seminarians, "If you're going to sin, don't be a sniveling little sinner! Be a big one!" Maybe. But people outside of Christ lack the cohesive power that holds life together. They live with an abandon but their lives produce decay and death. The saints possess the gospel which is the salvation both of society and of the individual. But too often they show none of the bubbling, springing joy that children of God should exhibit before the world.

Ken Anderson has a bit of pungent poetry that goes like this:

> Said Parson Wry, in a moment of mirth
>   And a moment of salient reasoning,
> There are many saints, the salt of the earth,
>   Who could do with a good bit more seasoning! [5]

The genuine follower of Jesus combines both the joy and the

conserving quality that holds society together and close to God. Let him who has ears to hear do a lot of hearing!

Years ago I read the story of a young Chinese Christian, Grace Wong, who came to America for her college education. One weekend she visited in the lovely home of a classmate. Perhaps there is no better way to learn the people of any land than by visits in their family groups. Grace Wong found the customs in that American home quite different from those practiced in her simple Oriental home. On that particular Sunday, the family took their guest for a picnic and a long drive over the beautiful countryside. They desired above all to give Grace a memorable day.

With characteristic courtesy but with some perplexity she questioned her friend about the family's behavior on that Sunday. "You will be so kind as to pardon me, but I am wondering how you know you belong to the church." Her friend replied that the family had always belonged to the church.

"But I am very much wanting to know how you are different," persisted little Grace Wong. "I cannot find what it is you do to be different. At home there are very many things that show us different. We do not smoke opium. We do not gamble. You play for prizes and would smoke rather than be thought queer. I cannot find what is the time when you read your Bibles together. My father uses our car each Sunday to take the people from our street to the mission church. You have a car and you have taken me, your guest, on a picnic and a day away from the church. It is not as if I think it all wrong, only I cannot see how you are different from those not belonging to Christ. I am only asking how you know you are a church member. What do you do to show you belong?"

That is a probing analysis! How would you give an answer? We have no problem accepting the idea that Christians, saved by the One whose name they bear, should be different from people who make no claim to the Savior. Our trouble comes when we are called upon *to do* his will, to show daily how we love him, to put into practice what we profess. People who live under the cross are going to be different in attitude, speech, acts, and spirit from men dominated by the world-spirit. Is this more than we can take? Thomas a Kempis' words are still accurate: "Jesus hath now many lovers of His heavenly kingdom, but few bearers of His Cross." [6] It is easier to admire Jesus than it is to follow him!

But Jesus calls us to "leave all and follow him." That is a call to radical obedience. Oddly enough, that obedience *to him brings an eternal joy!* The cross that speaks of death is combined with resurrection. Thus that cross is transformed so that it becomes a sign of victory. Had you ever noticed that Jesus' promises of joy came just prior to the cross? This joy is something far removed from mere hedonistic delights based on surface living. The Christian dies to self and lives for others in Christ's name. He learns this from his Master, who "for the joy that was set before him endured the cross" (Heb. 12:2, RSV). Dora Byron contrasts his cross and hers in this poem:

> His cross was but a common thing of cypress wood.
> Upon a tired hill, desolate it stood;
> And yet its arms have reached from sea to sea,
> Arms so strong that they have set men free;
> And love so bright burning long ago
> Changed the cross to gold with its glow.
> My cross sometimes is a weary thing, too hard to bear,
> A tiny, ugly thing; it floods my soul in hopeless care!
> But with His love I, too, will make that cross of gold,
> And pour the dark, tear-stained wood into His mould.
> My cross can never stretch its arms from sea to sea,
> But it can raise my heart to God and set me free.

2
Discipleship: Impulsive or Reflective?

Luke 9:57-62; 14:25-33

A widely heralded evangelistic crusade had come and gone. Under the open skies, thousands of people made "decisions for Christ." I am not qualified to determine the merit or lasting quality of those responses to the simple appeals made by the evangelist. God alone reads the human heart.

One thing I do know: In a crusade at a football stadium it is easier to make a response than it is in a church before people who know us and who will scrutinize our lives after the response has been made. In either case follow-up work is essential if converts are to be strengthened, instructed, and integrated into the fellowship of the church. During this period it may become apparent that some persons have followed Christ impulsively, not reflectively. Their initial response to him lacked depth of understanding. Would a fuller awareness of Christ's claims have turned them off rather than pulled them in?

For nothing is clearer than the fact that Jesus' expectations for his followers are high and demanding. He puts the case to us rather bluntly for he wants no superficial response, no half-hearted disciple. In this age of cheap grace and easy church membership, his teaching on discipleship may fall on deaf ears.

But we are obligated, if we take him seriously, to let persons know what they are getting into when they decide to follow him. Otherwise, they may share the shock of a youth who had joined a church and had just received a copy of the church covenant. He literally exploded! "Nobody ever told me I'd have to do all those things!" he cried. When I heard this, I began to wonder what would happen in the churches if the covenant should be read just before the invitation to discipleship!

Jesus, you see, imposes ultimate demands upon his followers. The cross which we bear in his name requires that we take those demands seriously. It calls for a reordering of our priorities.

The cross with its call to Christocentric living takes *priority over self*. "If any man would come after me, let him deny himself and take up his cross daily and follow me." "If any one comes to me and does not hate . . . his own life he cannot be my disciple" (Luke 9:23; 14:26, RSV). The key thought in these striking verses has to do with self-denial or self-renunciation. Perhaps all of us practice some form of renunciation whether it is a good thing or an evil thing that we surrender. We are always giving up something. But what does it mean to give up self?

What Jesus has in mind is not the substitution of one thing for another, like a man "sacrificing" a Cadillac for a Chevrolet! He points to the self, the center of our being. That must yield completely to Christ. Do you think that such comes easily? The very last citadel to fall is the self-centered self! Eugenia Price recalls how hard it was for her to surrender the whole of self to Christ. Converted in her early adult years, this cultured and capable woman found her "old" nature rising up frequently to challenge her new center for living, Christ. From Paul she had learned that self must die, but in her experience she discovered that self refused to stay dead.[1]

"With Christ you died," cried Paul (Col. 2:20, RSV). Your life is now "hid with Christ in God" (3:3). What emerges is a new creation (2 Cor. 5:17), though some elements of the old life must still be "put to death" (Col. 3:5-10). Changes in the self do not come cheap or easy. There is the pain of a birth experience; there is the trauma of dying. "I have been crucified with Christ; it is no longer I who live, but Christ who lives in me; and the life I now live in the flesh I live by faith in the Son of God, who loved me and gave himself for me" (Gal. 2:20). Self is not annihilated or swallowed up. But it is transformed. The life once bent on self-satisfaction, dominated by self-love, and directed by self-will is now Christ-centered and God-directed.

Alfred Tennyson wrote:

> Love took up the harp of Life, and smote on
>   all the chords with might;
> Smote the chord of Self, that, trembling,
>   passed in music out of sight.

Self yields to a new master. Men once bent on the chief seats in the kingdom now settle for a cup of pain and a baptism of suffering. They are now willing to follow Christ as servants rather than sit beside him as lieutenants. If you think that this requires self-contempt, you are mistaken. Self-respect is a characteristic of Christ's followers. But the self we respect is one transformed by Christ. Its whole stance toward the Master is bound up in the prayer of obedience: "Not my will but thine be done." Could anything short of a miracle bring us to such dedication to Christ? George Matheson caught the vision of that dedication in his famous hymn:

> O cross that liftest up my head,
>   I dare not ask to hide from thee,
> I lay in dust life's glory dead,
> And from the ground there blossoms red
>   Life that shall endless be.

The cross takes *priority over our human attainments and posses-sions.* Our material wealth and life's trappings furnish us a grand opportunity for serving effectively as Christ's followers. Or they prove a hindrance to the bearing of the cross. Try, if you can, to catch the thrust of Jesus' words: "Whoever of you does not renounce all that he has cannot be my disciple." Let a man surrounded by his achievements and economic securities hear the challenging question, "Do you love me more than these?" (John 21:15, RSV). In an age that attaches excessive value to money, goods, public acclaim, and other transient possessions, how are we to take Jesus' ultimate demand?

A rich young ruler once presented himself to Jesus. "Good Teacher, what must I do to inherit eternal life?" (Mark 10:17, RSV). That is a worthy and searching question. It is one that multitudes of sincere young people are asking in our own day. How did Jesus answer that youth? He tested his earnestness and readiness to accept the way leading to eternal life. "Go, sell what you have, and give to the poor, and you will have treasure in heaven; and come, follow me" (v. 21, RSV). First of all, you see, Jesus gave him opportunity to honor God and help persons through a sharing of his wealth. In your case, something other than money may be involved. In either instance Christ asks us to follow him on *his* terms, not our own.

Jesus, you see, will not lower the demands of the Kingdom to get halfhearted, partially committed followers. Money or its equivalent may stand as a barrier to our full dedication to the Master. Because of an idolatrous attachment to things—not neces-sarily evil in themselves—we may turn away from Christ as did that young ruler. Or we may play the game of trying to hold onto Christ and our idols at the same time.

For in an affluent society such as ours, how do well-to-do people "leave all to follow Christ?" If they dispose of all their economic securities, who would then support them and their families? And is there no validity to the view that we can hold those goods and minister to others in Christ's name? I would not like to tone down or explain away Jesus' demands. But I do believe that he used a shock treatment on that young ruler. Often he has to shatter our pride, puncture our illusions of goodness, and disturb our settled complacency. Only then do we give him full attention and full obedience.

May not wealth, culture, academic degrees, station in life, and access to power be put into service for Christ? They can be if the commitment of self to him is authentic. "First they gave themselves to the Lord," said Paul of those poverty-stricken Macedonian Christians and their sacrificial giving (2 Cor. 8:5). What we call stewardship is simply the expression of an inner devotion to Christ. And it shows itself in the whole of life.

No one would object to a rich person's disposition to remember religious institutions and causes in his will. But why should a man deny his wealth to such causes while he is alive? God wants the man and his money during that man's earthly existence. Perhaps the real problem, as in the case of the young ruler, is that of a fixed self-centeredness. The freeing of the self may open the door to generous giving. When we are yielded to Christ, it is not difficult to dedicate our resources for concerns close to his heart.

Persons who complain about Christ's total demands may be defective in their discipleship. They lack a clear understanding of the Gospels or the will to obey the Master's mandate. To follow him is to take up our cross *daily*, to bring life at every moment under his discipline. This means not occasional acts of piety or momentary bursts of enthusiasm but a steadfast loyalty to Christ's claims upon us.

Jesus' cross, so Ralph Cushman notes, is the proper vantage point for an analysis of our commitment.

> Ah, when I look up at the cross
> Where God's great Steward suffered loss—
> Yes, loss of life and blood for me!
> A trifling thing it seems to be
> To pay the tithe, dear Lord, to thee,
> Of time or talent, wealth or store—
> Full well I know I owe Thee more;
> A million times I owe Thee more!
> But that is just the reason why
> I lift my heart to God on high
> And pledge Thee by this portion small,
> My life, my love, my all in all!
> This holy token at thy cross
> I know, as gold, must seem but dross,
> But in my heart, Lord, thou dost see
> How it has pledged my all to Thee,
> That I a steward true may be! [2]

The cross *takes priority over all human relationships.* Here Jesus' words become altogether unbearable to our modern ears! "If any one comes to me and does not hate his own father and mother and wife and children and brothers and sisters, . . . he cannot be my disciple." Many people have stumbled at Jesus' words about "hating" one's closest relatives. But the Greek word translated "hate" can mean "to put in second place." This is the essential meaning of the parallel passage in Matthew (10:37). Even so we must not miss the powerful claim that Jesus puts before his hearers. Admittedly he sanctioned family loyalty and despised any attempts to get around the responsible care of a man's loved ones (Matt. 15:3-6; cf. 1 Tim. 5:8). At the same time he would not allow any rival to himself for first place in our hearts.

Here we need to note something most important. Persons who exalt Christ in their lives will love their families not less but more. Christ in us sanctifies our homelife and the love he puts in us cleanses and strengthens human relationships. Genuinely Christian people are equipped in spirit and character to love, respect, and live honorably with those who share life at close range.

Christ's followers should make good family members. Generally, persons who exalt him in their hearts and seriously seek to live by his teachings are worthy of trust. A young man once proposed to a lovely girl in a strange manner. Said he, "Honey, I want to marry you. And I promise you I'll always give you the second place in my heart." Her dark eyes snapped and she prepared to tell him off! No young woman desires a second place in her man's heart! Then she realized that the man proposing to her was a committed Christian. For him the primary loyalty belonged to Jesus Christ. She concluded that she could trust herself to a man who loved Christ above everything else.

Sometimes loyalty to Jesus requires a painful course of action. There are instances when a disciple stands alone in his own home. Other family members may scoff at Christ or simply ignore him and his church. The follower of Christ gets no encouragement or support in his response to the Master. A family may be a drag on one's faith. Jesus foresaw situations when homes might be sharply divided because of him (Matt. 10:34-36).

Early in his life, Harold Schaly, a native of Brazil and now a Baptist pastor there, encountered sharp emotional disruption in his household. Born into a devout Catholic home, he served as altar boy in his church. But one day he came under the influence of a Protestant missionary, heard the gospel of redeeming love, and finally received Christ as his Savior. His family reacted bitterly to the news, and reminded him that he could be thrown out of the Catholic Church and his home should he follow through in baptism. For days he wrestled with this problem. Then the words of Jesus crossed his young mind: "Every one who acknowledges me before men, I also will acknowledge before my Father who is in heaven; but whoever denies me before men, I also will deny before my Father who is in heaven" (Matt. 10:32-33, RSV). That settled the matter for him. But, said he, "The hardest thing I ever had to do was to tell my weeping, heartbroken mother good-bye." Yet he did just that.

There is a happy sequel to that story. Harold came to the United States for college and seminary training. Back in Brazil as a missionary pastor, he was able to win his mother and some other family members to Christ. The point, however, is that when he faced a choice between his family and Christ, he chose to follow Jesus. For you, a choice for the Master may entail no such cleavage between love of family and loyalty to Jesus. But do not forget that he demands first place in your heart even though that proves costly.

We have seen that, according to Christ, every contending claim upon us must yield to his lordship. Does it surprise us that *Jesus cautions his hearers about superficial, impulsive discipleship?* So statistically oriented are we that success even in the kingdom is reckoned in terms of numbers. Now here is Jesus rebuking hollow, impulsive promises of discipleship. God wants men and women who will continue loyal to him. A sound, durable marriage requires a great deal more than the impulse to wed! And partial commitments to Christ invite failure and provoke the mockery of godless souls (Ps. 1:1).

Our discipleship involves far more than a warm, emotional response to Jesus. It calls for a realistic appraisal of the enemy's strength and our willingness to take the field against him. Is this not the point of the short parables drawn from military life and the building trade? In effect Jesus is saying, "Discipleship is costly. Enter upon it with eyes wide open. Be sure you commit your whole self to me. The cross demands all that you are." This does not mean that I wait to become a disciple until I know I can hold out! But it does mean that I understand the seriousness of discipleship and a readiness to take all its risks.

Bearing the cross brings out the best that is in us. That cross is a center about which we rally our energies. It is not a drug to soothe our nerves or a palliative to cure all little ills. The cross is a powerful bludgeon, not a soft cue tip to massage our sores. Christ's cross was coarse and rough. No smooth little gold cross will frighten Satan! Our cross is demanding. For it requires that self-sacrificial love which is discipleship's unique mark. "Take up the cross and follow me!" This is an invitation to live. It is also a ringing call to share Christ's mission among men. We hear the call and we take action. And we follow him close up, not at some comfortable, safe distance!

3
The Disciple's Witness

Luke 24:45-49

Some time ago I visited a couple who had experienced considerable reverses, including long-term illnesses. For over thirty minutes I listened to a doleful story, interspersed with bitter comments about other persons. As I listened I wondered, "Do they know any good news at all? After all the years of living, have they no joys to share, no good things to tell?"

That experience is not unlike our encounter with the daily newspapers! Wading through all the tales of crime and trouble and natural calamities, one feels like crying aloud, "Does nothing good ever happen in our world?" Of course the daily news is a frightful commentary on the state of natural man. Hence the sensible dictum of Karl Barth that the Christian should face the day with the newspaper in one hand and the Bible in the other!

The Bible is fully realistic in its appraisal of life's realities. But it also contains a gospel, good news about God's love and design for man. Of all persons, the Christian has heard, received, and rejoiced in that gospel. And he has the lifelong privilege of sharing it with his contemporaries. Witnessing, in the sense that Jesus intended, is a fundamental part of Christian discipleship.

There are certain things about this witness to the gospel that we need to set in focus.

First of all, *the object of our witness is man himself.* Quite correctly, this age has been called the age of man, for attention has focused upon him as it once centered upon God! But the gospel also concerns itself with man—and in the name of man's Redeemer, so must we.

There is evidence that man's self-centered focus has brought about some human miseries that he cannot manage. The gods whom he worships invariably let him down. They have no help to offer him when he exhausts his round of diversion or bumps up against tragedy, emptiness, and death!

What does one do when he discovers that he has no purpose in life? The god of materialism, for example, alienates parents and children and makes homes an outpost of hell on earth! I read recently of an educated youth, son of a multimillionaire, who posed as a bum and spent a summer among "down and outs" in a city slum. He was searching for something, trying to get away from a wealthy but intolerable life that failed to evoke his sense of humanity. In less dramatic fashion, that youth's quest and experience has been duplicated in the lives of countless others.

Our age speaks often of identity crisis. Like the prodigal son of Jesus' parable, many persons are restless, lonely, with confused self-images. They do not know who they are, what they should do with themselves, or to whom they might turn for help. In an era of skepticism, multitudes have no belief in anything beyond the tomb. Man comes forth from the unknown and shortly passes away into the unknown. So some reason and so many fear.

Something of pathos appears in the life of a person who cannot identify with his past or who discovers at physical maturity that he does not know who his biological parents are. In his book, *Magnolia Jungle,* the author P. D. East reflects upon the jolt he received in his late teens on discovering that he could not establish his parental identity at all. With this critical situation as illustration, let me say that we are not left here as spiritual orphans! We have an identity as sons of the Father God and need not feel lost in this expansive universe. (See John 14:16-21).

Man is always searching for something on which to stand, some fixed point, some enduring and well-based hope. Sometimes his speech betrays his despair and longing. The existential writer, Albert Camus, speaking to a group of Dominican monks, said, "I share with you the same revulsion from evil. But I do not share your hope, and I continue to struggle against this universe in which children suffer and die." [1] One appreciates the honesty of this man even as he detects the despair in his speech.

Does despair and the sense of utter helplessness lead men to turn their faces God-ward? George Herbert, the English poet, once asserted that God gave men every gift but rest. He withheld that so that its very absence would drive men to his breast. [2] It does appear that, driven to the limit, man sometimes turns toward God.

Are we so made that, as Augustine noted, our restless hearts find no rest until they rest in him? That our minds respond to the deep that is God? "Deep calls unto deep." Professor Adam Schaff, a famous communist philosopher, was speaking before a student group at Warsaw University in Poland. A serious student, steeped in the teaching that there is no God, that religion is an "opiate of the people," dropped an intellectual bombshell as he timidly put the question to the lecturer. "Please don't be angry, but could you explain the meaning of life, sir?" It was a disturbing question, but a valid one as the professor himself noted. "As long as people die, suffer, lose their loved ones," said he, "just so long will questions about the meaning of life have full rights." [3]

The judgment of God, it seems, consists in part of that emptiness and sickness we experience as a consequence of missing the point of living. We have to live in our dirt, disease, loneliness, and fear. And unfortunately we infect others! C. S. Lewis, reflecting on the possibility of life on other planets, rather hopes that we find no rational beings there. Earth man is such a deceiver, a cheat, an exploiter and exterminator of all that he meets, says Mr. Lewis. He charges that "We are not fit yet to visit other worlds. We have filled our own with massacre, torture, syphilis, famine, dust bowls, and with all that is hideous to the ear or eye. Must we go on to infect new realms?" [4]

Those are words of indictment. They hurt because they are so true. But we do not have to stay so lost, undone, and broken. For God has come into our world, taken on the form of man, and dwelt among us full of grace and truth. We face the *truth* and it is hard to bear! We receive the *grace* and we can become sons of the Father. That is good news indeed! And it is our business to share it with others.

The subject of our witness is Christ. You and I have one word to proclaim, one person to acknowledge before men. We must discover what this means—and what it does not mean.

There are some fallacies about witnessing that need to be faced. Our witness is not concerned with a body of doctrines or set beliefs. To require another person just to believe a group of propositions may even prevent his putting faith in Jesus Christ! To be hooked on a method or a plan for witnessing may cause one to obscure the One concerning whom we witness.

Nor is our witness some form of church promotion, whether we are plugging the pastor, the institution, or the fellowship. These are easy substitutes for our true witness.

The witness to Christ must not be construed as pushing through reforms, adopting social applications, projecting causes which, though the fruits of Christian living, are not the central witness. We need to clear up one other point. The term *soul-winning* has often replaced Jesus' term, *witness*. A successful soul-winner, like a skilled Indian warrior, is expected to bring back "trophies for the Chief!" I do not intend a caricature, for I am grateful for serious, devoted personal workers who do win people to Christ. Jesus, however, only commands us—all of us—to proclaim the essential message of salvation. God will handle the computer—he will count up the results, indeed will grant them. We are to witness, not to bother about arithmetic! The witness tells what he has seen, what he knows, what he builds his own life upon.

The witness is concerned with the good news concerning God's deed of redemption. Through the One who died and arose, two facts may be proclaimed.

There is the fact of *repentance*. Repentance is man's response to the Spirit's conviction of sin, his powerful indictment of our guilty souls. For he does convict the world of sin, righteousness, and judgment (John 16:8). On every account we are condemned! But God's mercy confronts us. He makes possible that new mind, new life, new way that repentance involves. Paul had the same sort of thing in mind when he spoke of the new creation in Christ (2 Cor. 5:17).

Repentance means a decisive break with the "old" way. It means the will to turn to God. And the sincerity of the repenting person is seen in his resolute purpose to please God as well as in the ethical fruits of his changed nature. It is this dynamic, transforming experience—a thing we know—that constitutes a part of our witness. To put it simply, you and I know someone who has been fundamentally changed through the power of God alone. We tell the unsaved person about that.

There is the fact of *forgiveness*. Put in psychological language, God gives us a sense of release from guilt's domination. We can accept the fact that he has accepted us. The wall of hostility has been torn down. An inner peace has come to my life. I now feel a new freedom, as though shackles had been broken from me. A power for thinking, affirming, and acting has come to my life.

All of this has come about because of a loving heavenly Father who has shown himself through the Man from Nazareth! Now I tell another of what has come to me! Jesus reminds us that our individual experience is a part of God's design for his whole creation. In other words, redemption is no sudden intruder—it is God's purpose in history (Luke 24:27,45 f.)! And its clear point of culmination came in Jesus Christ!

My witness moves from my own subjective experience to the fact of my Savior! I do not simply recount my own story, nor do I suggest that every man's response to Christ be like my own. Ultimately, the spotlight is not on me but on him! For Jesus, not this man, is the vital element in our evangelistic witness. It is "in his name" that men are approached, confronted, and won.

The medium of the witness, however, is a human life and voice. This fact leaps out of the New Testament records repeatedly. The early Christians were called many things: brothers, believers, disciples, servants, saints, people of God. Whatever their designation, they bore one common commission: Witness faithfully to God's loving action in Jesus Christ.

We declare good news! That which we have received, tasted, known, and to which we have yielded our lives—this is what we proclaim. We declare not the result of our long and painstaking search—rather we proclaim one who found us and loved us and won us. We cried out of our lostness, bewilderment, and hunger, and he heard us. We have discovered in him the peace and strength that this world could never furnish. He called us from darkness to light, from superficial activities to share the timeless life of God. Now we say to all men, "This can be your Christ; for the difference between you and me is the difference he can make."

If it is true that he can make life over again, that is the grandest news ever heard!

Will you observe the inclusiveness of Jesus' plain words: All of his followers are called to be "witnesses to these things." The proclaimer is a herald, declaring news that he has received. Elsewhere, we find Paul also referring to the inclusive task of Christians as he calls upon us all to be ministers of reconciliation. It is time for us to read the New Testament as it is written. There is not "the preacher" and a lot of lay members in the church. "The preacher," as sole proclaimer and custodian of morality and the Bible is a misnomer. (While we are questioning terms, let me include the word *reverend*. Who is reverend and holy? Only God, I assume! There are good New Testament terms like pastor or minister that we can use to describe God-given functions.) But none of us, pastors or lay persons, are exempt from the call to be witnesses. How could the nations of the earth come to know the risen Lord apart from the multiple witness?

God has put the "liberating keys" in the hands of every confessing believer! Gabriel Marcel speaks with force: "Conversion is the act by which man is called to become a witness." [5] He contends that anyone capable of commitment is capable of bearing witness, and that each person must reveal the light as God gave it to him. This is in line with Jesus' own words: "Let your light so shine before men, that they may see your good works and give glory to your Father who is in heaven" (Matt. 5:16). We form a task force in the world. Not just a few professionals, but the whole band of believers. This forms God's spearhead into society, permeating and penetrating, and making the Spirit of Christ known and realized in action.

The witness must be verbally given, not just nonverbally shown in our lives. The idea that all we are required to do is live good, clean lives so Christ can shine through us is false! At least, it is not the whole of witnessing. On the stand, the witness gives a verbal account; he does not merely sit in the witness chair and look good or knowledgeable.

Why are the saints so silent about Jesus Christ? Is it because we are without words or experience concerning him? Our world puts lots of stress on *witnessing*. A few hours with television discloses the fact that every kind of trick is being used to give testimony to products men would sell. It is done verbally as well as nonverbally. And there are religious sects as well as articulate radio preachers who are extremely vocal while we are silent.

Sometimes I think modern churchmen are caught on the horns of a dilemma. Two fears plague us: there is the fear that we will not be regarded respectable and "religious" enough, and there is the fear that we shall be adjudged too pious! This latter fear keeps us from talking about our own personal awareness of Christ or our best understanding of the Bible.

Then, too, this is the era of the *tentative*, the *uncertain*, the *maybe*. A student director in a university setting recently, in commenting on the ministerial dropouts of his theological age-group, noted that many seemed unsure of themselves or their functions in life or their own beliefs. Said he somewhat sadly, "So seldom do we hear a man who believes and strongly enunciates his convictions." A solid witness needs to do both! One may hold noble beliefs and live a sincere good life. But these are only background for actual witness—they are never substitutes for it. And if faith is genuine, it can be shared. If it is never shared, does one have it at all?

Words possess power to burn their way into the mind. They stir emotions and challenge the will. Witnessing is concerned with the Word itself, the Word made flesh, God's communication with men. It is still his plan that men verbalize their faith. When he wants to get things done, he clothes himself with a living, articulate, committed person. *Persons* are his witnesses in the world. And there are always too few of them, despite the armies of enrolled church members. Will you recall that when Jesus urged his disciples to pray for laborers for the harvest, because there were so few, he was surrounded by a host of "church" folks? He would find the same situation now!

The witness never goes alone. He is no solitary hunter setting out on a safari! Jesus was withdrawing his physical presence from his followers. But he promised them and the church through the centuries a power that would carry them along. "Behold, I send the promise of my Father upon you; but stay in the city, until you are clothed with power from on high" (Luke 24:49, RSV). "You shall receive power when the Holy Spirit has come upon you; and you shall be my witnesses in Jerusalem and in all Judea and Samaria and to the end of the earth" (Acts 1:8).

The mysteries of God elude our little minds. But the assurances of God can be known experientially though we fail to fathom them intellectually. Some of earth's plain people have been its most potent witnesses, for they have been undergirded and infused with a power that was given from above. It is this inflowing energy that gives joy to the believer, brings courage to the timid, enables communication to the unsaved, and fills life with a sense of purpose.

4
Disciples in the Making
Matthew 28:16-20

"Christians should not close the door on any hope of finding a new foundation for the life of the self-tormented human race." Thus spoke Winston Churchill in an address delivered at Edinburgh shortly after the ending of World War II. His appeal for the use of human wisdom in exploring bases for a more peaceful world order has often fallen on deaf ears.

But can human wisdom alone cope with those enormous world problems that seem to baffle our best minds? Such complex problems defy simple analysis. Nor do they yield to easy, single-track solutions. Where, then, do we find a door of hope?

Certainly the answer to that question lies not in religious clichés which we toss around so glibly. Nor does it consist in some rearrangement of social structures or a wider diffusion of technology's vast benefits. Is there some other way of getting at the root problems that tear men and nations apart? Can we reasonably expect to find help in following Jesus' strategy, disclosed in what we sometimes describe as the Great Commission?

In the face of human poverty, fear, distress, and lostness, Jesus boldly assigned his followers a mission that is worldwide and destined to be world-changing. His words may sound incredibly idealistic, if not foolish, to our generation. Possibly they sounded the same to his first disciples. Before them lay the vast Roman Empire and beyond that the rest of a world they never expected to see, much less to evangelize.

"Go therefore," they heard Jesus say, "and make disciples of all nations." How bold and incredible were those words! Yet they introduce us to the Master's key strategy. The entire passage (Matt. 28:18-20) is crucial but the central affirmation is the injunction to "make disciples." Indeed, this is the only imperative statement that occurs in the Greek text. The English translations have "go," "baptize," and "teach" but in the Greek these come on as participles.

Evidently *Jesus directed the active energies of the church toward the making of disciples.* The point of our "going" is to introduce persons to Jesus Christ and to enable them to hear his summons to "follow me." We may carry out this mission in various ways, according to the nature and needs of people. Without question the persons who do this going, the ones whom Jesus addresses, have themselves been transformed by God's grace. They give sincere witness to a holy love that has reached them and released them from the bondage of sin. The beginning point in making disciples is the winning of individuals to the One we ourselves have come to know experientially.

But this is only the beginning, not the end. It is never enough just to win recruits. An army does far more than enroll or enlist individuals. Important battles are not won with padded rolls or raw recruits. Jesus' strategy goes much deeper than collecting signed commitment cards and presenting candidates for baptism. Does not his example of training his followers throw light upon the process of making disciples? He brought men into a close fellowship with himself, gave them specific instruction, demonstrated ways of doing things, sent them out to try their own hand at preaching and healing, then allowed them on returning to share their experience. (See Luke 9:1-17,37-43; 10:1-17.)

That Jesus saw the universal scope of his church's mission is apparent in the words, "make disciples of all nations." On the strength of this statement, we rightly develop worldwide missionary concerns and encourage local churches to support those concerns. Christian missions, however, must not be seen as a separate function but as a fundamental part of the church's effort at making disciples. What Jesus seems to insist upon is that the whole world is our field—long before John Wesley's claim that the world was his parish!

Disciples are made by other disciples. So far as I know this privilege is not denied to any Christian. We are all ministers in the deepest sense of that word. And we desperately need to put our gifts to work for Christ if the church is to carry out the magnitude of its discipling task. Is this not suggested by Paul's classic statement in Ephesians? "It was he who gave some to be apostles, some to be prophets, some to be evangelists, and some to be pastors and teachers, to prepare God's people for works of service, so that the body of Christ may be built up" (Eph. 4:11-12, NIV).[1]

Disciple-making is the church's big responsibility. And the church's leadership is enjoined to make certain that this responsibility is carried out.

Authentic discipleship involves a careful and constant obedience to Christ's commands. Emil Brunner once noted that for the Christian there are no moral holidays. This never means a joyless sort of existence. Indeed, the life of obedience is characterized by a joy so deep that Jesus described it as blessedness (Matt. 5:3-12). In bondage to Christ we are of all persons most free.

The nature of our obedience is clear: "All that I have com-

manded." The church's responsibility—or the responsibility of
mature disciples who do the teaching—is equally clear: "Teaching
them to observe." Look for a moment at the role of the church
in teaching.

From the outset the Christian community has been a fellowship
of learning. Devotion to "the apostles teaching" (Acts 2:42) characterized the early church. This instruction was particularly important for new converts who had emerged from a permissive
pagan culture. There are evidences that the New Testament
churches developed a body of instruction somewhat like a cate-
chism. By the second century, there arose a manual or set of
teaching called the Didache. This provided moral guidance for
those young in the faith.

Do we lay to heart Jesus' command that we teach his followers
the content and the meaning of his message? Or do we assume
that beginners in the Christian faith will grow without this kind
of special feeding? What Jesus commands is a knowledge of his
teaching. We may wonder what he means by the words, "all
that I have commanded you." Until wonderment ceases, we might
examine his ethical teachings, his words about love, the counsel
found in parables and precepts. The Four Gospels, though they
record only a part of his total teaching, form a curriculum which
we are not likely to exhaust.

But Jesus envisions more than a band of disciples with heads
full of knowledge. We are "to observe" all that he has commanded!
The Greek word translated "observe" means to guard or preserve
a thing. But it also means to *practice* a thing, not simply to believe
or to preserve it. We are not here presented with options. Professor
John Knox once wrote that above all else Jesus meant for his
ethical teaching to be taken most seriously.[2] The same could be
said of Jesus' commission to his followers. We are to learn his
commands, live by them faithfully, and encourage others to do

the same. When Christ utters a command, we have no alternative but to obey. Granted, the shape of our obedience is sometimes difficult to determine and often even more difficult to accept. But we were never lured by a Christ who offered us an easy path or a simple way. When we come under his yoke (Matt. 11:29), we submit to his requirements. They are right for us because he himself makes them. And the yoke can become a cross!

Biblical illiteracy and defective discipleship are common weaknesses within modern Christendom. Undoubtedly there are many reasons for this: the secularization of life, the repudiation of Christian norms, the church's obsession with numbers and power, ineffective teaching, and inept preaching. Sensitive Christian leaders rightly urge a full-orbed evangelism that includes the call to discipleship and the growth of converts in the Christian life. A wise deacon in one of our fast-growing churches stated this concern. Said he, "We have reached a lot of people for which I am grateful. But we have not developed them doctrinally or ethically. Now we must teach this diverse group the meaning of Christian beliefs and the dimensions of Christian responsibility." May his tribe increase!

Discipleship and the command to make disciples can never be regarded as peripheral concerns. They are central and basic, related to the vitality and continuing mission of the church itself. Even more, *they come to us from One who has ultimate authority.* What we have therefore is not simply a workable plan devised by a council or a committee. Councils and committees may wrestle with the meaning of the command, but the source of that mandate is Jesus Christ himself. "All authority in heaven and on earth has been given to me. Go therefore and make disciples of all nations."

Jesus' claim to "every form of authority" belongs in the category of his other claims (see, for example, Matt. 11:27-30; 12:6-8;

16:18-19; John 6:35,44; 8:12; 10:30; 11:25-26; 12:32; 18:37). What are we to make of them? We may dismiss them as the exaggerated claims of a misguided zealot. We may glibly assent to them but never really allow them to alter our patterns of behavior. Or we may take Jesus at his word, accept the truthfulness of his claim, and spend our days trying to fulfill his command.

Jesus, so George Buttrick says, is the absolute authority in matters of religion. He has spoken *the* word about our human natures: we are lost without God, yet we are intended for his Kingdom and he seeks us through Jesus. Jesus has spoken *the* word about salvation: He himself is God coming to die in our stead, reconciling us to the Father, saving us from eternal death, releasing us to live now. Jesus has spoken *the* word about human destiny: Men are more than mere flesh—they are called to be children of God. Jesus has spoken *the* word about God: He is a loving Father.[3] I would add the fact that Jesus has spoken *the* word about Christian living: we are called to be lifelong disciples, obedient to the Master's commands, moving under his authority.

Is it God who has bestowed upon Jesus such inclusive authority? Was it the quality of his life that merited such authority? Yes, but even more his unbroken relationship with God, and his obedience unto death. But he comes to us as one who could not be contained by death's powers. God has raised him from the dead, so the New Testament and the Christian centuries affirm (see Acts 2:23-24; 3:14-15). He now bears the keys of experience and authority (Rev. 1:18). Paul could think of him as the cosmic Christ through whom all things were created, the one whose image was ultimately to be stamped upon all creation (Col. 1:15-20). We come to him with great confidence for he is in full command of all the means necessary "for the expansion of his Kingdom."

It is this authority of the living Christ which undergirds the command to make disciples. And it is his authority and power which form the basis of all true discipleship. Baptism, among other things, is an outward sign of our willingness to take on the life of discipleship. It is our open declaration of identity with the living, authoritative Christ. He who has saved us has the right to command us.

Disciples are to make disciples. But not in their own power or by their ingenuity alone. For in it all we are *sustained and directed by a living presence.* The help we need is provided by One who abides with us and is in us. "I am with you always, to the close of the age." He enables us to live out our discipleship. And he goes with us on our mission to make disciples of others.

These words of our Lord constitute a precious promise. They bring us assurance that he is with us in our daily experiences. He is not detached from our lives, not bound to a given place, not frozen in time or prisoned in a creed, not limited even to the best of all books. He is gloriously alive in our world. He is known to us in our personal experiences, and is the source of our energy and enlightenment. And he comes close to us as we walk in obedience, as we minister and witness to others, as we seek to bring hope and righteousness to some corner of our world. The German pastor-theologian, Helmut Thielicke, claims that "Jesus Christ is known only in discipleship, or He is not known at all." [4] Experiential knowledge like that is better than a thousand neatly framed arguments!

Jesus' promise comes not simply to individuals and not merely for our personal comfort. His words are addressed to a group, and may be most fittingly applied to the church in every generation. The living presence and the sustaining power equip us for our mission. What does Jesus mean by the words, "I am with you always"? Quite clearly, he is referring to the Holy Spirit who came in great power at Pentecost and who has been carrying forward the work of Christ through the Christian centuries. Christ is with us—in the Spirit. Is this not what he promised us in the Gospel of John? The Holy Spirit was to continue the message and ministry of Jesus (John 14:16-17,25; 15:26; 16:7-11,13-14), to keep alive the Presence.

Accordingly, Jesus urged his followers to wait for that infusion of power which the Spirit brings (Luke 24:49; Acts 1:8). "Clothed with power from on high" (immersed or enveloped in the Spirit's power), they would have strength for witnessing and making disciples. The work of the Spirit is thus a continuation of Jesus' work, not a departure from it. The Spirit communicates a sense of Christ's presence, not so much for our personal enjoyment as for our steadfast devotion to Christian discipleship. Ray Summers aptly notes that the Holy Spirit's coming enables us to discern the real meaning of bearing the cross and following after Christ.[5] And it is under the Spirit's direction that we know the freedom and joy that comes to the children of God (John 8:31-32,36; 5:11; 2 Cor. 3:17).

Although under the discipline of the cross, the disciple is most free. Though a bond slave of Christ, he walks in the freedom of the Spirit. He neither welcomes nor imposes on others a theological straitjacket or a legalistic code. He is never free from agonizing decisions or detached from life's critical issues. But he moves about freely, hopefully, enthusiastically. For Another walks with him.

Perhaps this is why T. W. Manson said that "the living Christ still has two hands, one to point the way, and the other held out to help us along." [6] I can not speak for you, but I myself daily need both those hands upon my life. For there is no release from the demands of discipleship, no lessening of his command for us to make disciples.

I have a feeling that Christ is more pleased with a *full* discipleship than filled sanctuaries or overflowing coffers. Possibly more attention to the first would have a redemptive influence on the others! One thing is certain: Jesus' mandate to discipleship remains. Do we dare test our churches in terms of obedience to that?

PART II

Experiencing Discipleship

5
Discipleship as Commitment

Mark 1:14-22

It had been a long hot night in the tropical climate of Galilee. Now the torches were doused and the boats beached. The night's toil was over. (Fishing is fun when it's a hobby, but it's work when it's a livelihood.) Birds were singing as if their throats would burst. The sea was calm—lapping at the graveled shore. The bright morning sun caused the men to squint their eyes when they looked toward the east. There was the smell of fish cooking and the color of bougainvillea in full bloom.

Andrew, tall and slender, stood in the stern of a boat facing the sunrise—and thinking the long, long thoughts of youth.

Andrew's elder brother, Simon, the senior partner in their fishing enterprise was squatting on the beach, repairing the nets. Dried sweat at his temples and his bald head made him look older than he was. He was bone-weary and oblivious to the beauty all around him. (It's strange how we take natural beauty for granted, especially when we live in the midst of it.)

Suddenly, Simon was startled at the crunch of gravel behind him. He turned his head, squinting as he looked up at the figure behind him. He recognized Jesus, the young rabbi from Nazareth. And then, he heard that commanding voice say, "Follow me and

47

I will make you become fishers of men" (Mark 1:17, RSV). Andrew and Simon had heard Jesus preach earlier. They had felt both intrigued and compelled by his message. Now there was no escaping a decision. The call of Jesus was both personal and specific. If they answered affirmatively, they would spend the rest of their lives learning what was involved in that simple invitation to follow the Christ.

Thus, Jesus called the kingdom's first recruits! They became his disciples or followers. A disciple is a student. The word means one who accepts and follows a teacher; one who is a pupil or learner.

THE CALL OF CHRIST CLAIMED THEM

Jesus took the initiative in calling the twelve. His voice sank like talons into their wills. They were claimed by Christ; staked out for kingdom purposes. Andrew and Simon, as well as others, abandoned their businesses to follow Jesus. (That sort of thing still occurs.) Jesus said they did not choose him, but "I have chosen you." The call of God to faith and discipleship still comes to persons at the divine initiative. Christ's unmistakable call can sustain a disciple when the going gets rough. He calls persons to faith and to follow.

Jesus *saw* Simon and Andrew, James and John. This word meant that he gazed intently at them. It was almost as though Jesus looked right into their hearts and motives. His spiritual insight perceived not only what they were but what their potential was as well. He saw more than fishermen—he saw apostles!

How do we look at people? What do we see when we look at them? Do we look at every person we meet with greedy eyes? Are they simply business prospects rather than persons to us?

When Jesus looks at us, he sees our motives and our love (or lack of it). He sees both what we are and what we can become.

It is the miracle of grace that God sees us as we are and loves us still. Surely one reason for this is that God also sees our potential.

Note that in this passage Jesus looked intently at Simon and called him to become a fisher of men. Remember also that later Peter denied Jesus within the high priest's house. Again Jesus turned and looked at Peter. That look from the Master broke the fisherman's heart and sent him out into the night weeping bitterly. Jesus looks at us repeatedly with both joy and disappointment.

Notice whom Jesus called! He called young people. Most of the twelve were young men, perhaps in their twenties or even younger. The missionary apostle Paul wrote years after the death of Jesus that there had been some five hundred disciples who saw Jesus ascend into heaven, "and the greater part remain unto this present." Jesus himself was a young man barely thirty years old. The original version of Isaac Watts' hymn, "When I Survey the Wondrous Cross," had a line which read, "On which the *young* Prince of Glory died." Jesus was young; and he understood youth with their anxiety and dreams, their temptations and their idealism.

Jesus also called different kinds of people. Peter was flamboyant. He had both a ready faith and a quick temper. John was a violent fellow who became a beloved spirit. Matthew was a collaborator with the Roman occupation troops; and Simon was a Zealot, a patriot sworn to drive the Romans out of Judea. Andrew had a clear faith and was always bringing others to Jesus. But faith came hard for Thomas and he was plagued with doubts. The disciples had very different personalities and backgrounds. Yet they were all men called to follow Jesus, and they were all used to help spread the gospel.

The same is true today. Jesus has attracted and called all sorts of persons. His church is made up of persons from every level of life: economic, cultural, social, and intellectual. Once I visited in a poor home where the husband and father had been sent to prison for robbery. He came to know Christ as Savior and today is a gospel minister and a highly useful citizen. Other examples could be cited to show that Jesus uses all kinds of persons as his disciples.

Why did Jesus call those men to be his disciples? He called them "to be with him." What higher honor can we imagine? They were to learn the Master as well as to learn what he would teach. They were to enjoy his companionship as well as hear his message.

Our faith is still essentially a personal relationship with the Christ. We place our ultimate faith not in a book or a doctrine, but in the man Jesus Christ.

Faith is more than intellectual belief. It is also a personal relationship and commitment. In the last analysis, our discipleship depends on nothing more than our love of Jesus Christ and our love of the persons for whom Christ died.

When Jesus left this earth physically, he left only two things behind—his blood on the ground and that small band of committed disciples. Christ's disciples have been faithful witnesses across the ages. Today there are reported to be one billion believers in the world—one fourth of the world's population!

The second reason for the disciples' call was that they might be "sent forth to preach." Devotional fellowship issues in practical sharing of our faith. They were called to be with Jesus and they were also called in order that they should go out and share their faith. Worship alone lacks practical expression. And doing good works without the deep roots of a devotional life lacks substance. Jesus called his disciples that they might be with him, *and* be sent out to share their faith.

A Call to Commitment

When Jesus called his disciples he said, "Follow me." He did not ask their intellectual assent alone, telling them what to think. Nor did he ask only for their emotional response, telling them how they should feel. These would come later. He asked their obedient faith: "Follow me." Their call was a divine invitation to pilgrimage, much like that of Abraham centuries before. Mark shows with sheer honesty what their reaction was: "As they followed, they were afraid" (Mark 10:32, KJV). It was an uncertain venture to which Jesus called them. So today our own pilgrimage in faith demands a certain risk factor.

A Call to Companionship

Jesus called the twelve to follow him. He did not say like Buddha, "This is the way, follow it." Rather, he said, "I am the way . . . follow me." It was a personal call.

Jesus gave the disciples a task. They were called not to an easy life but to one of service. He promised, "I will make you . . . " The call was open-ended. He said he would make them "fishers of men." Note that he started on the level where they were.

Ted Adams told about a visit to Silver Springs, Florida, where he watched fish swimming in their habitat beneath the glass-bottom boats. He said that when you fish for fish you bring them from life to death. However, when you fish for men, you bring them from death to life. Those without Christ are already dead in trespasses and sin. To "fish" for them, to win them to faith in Christ is to bring them to *new* life, indeed.

We have many motives for witnessing to our faith. Surely none are stronger than these two: our neighbor's desperate need and Christ's clear command. Therefore, witnessing is not an elective. It is not optional; it is every Christian's calling.

THE DISCIPLE'S ALTERNATIVE

Let us be perfectly honest. One does not have to become Christ's

disciple. While God graciously offers us salvation, we may accept
it or reject it. The rich young ruler chose not to follow Jesus
(Matt. 19:16-22). Others made this choice in response to Jesus'
personal ministry, "They did not believe in him" (see John 12:37-
40). It is possible today for persons to choose darkness rather
than light, because their deeds are evil. Lady Macbeth said about
the murder of King Duncan:

> Come thick night, and pall thee in the dunnest
>   smoke of hell,
> That my keen knife see not the wound it makes,
> Nor heaven peep through the blanket of the dark
> To cry, "Hold! Hold!"

This is a world in which persons can be eternally lost!

Just as honestly, however, we should also note that unbelief
is a heavy burden. It makes poor sense to be "without God, without
hope in the world." To remain in sin is a choice to remain an
orphan, without a heavenly Father. A person without Christ is
on life's long journey into eternal night. Such a life faces a bleak
abyss of nothingness—or worse.

Without faith in Christ, the future is bleak indeed: this stupid,
warring world is destined to be a mere cemetery. Unfaith must
be an unbearably heavy burden!

Some do not become Jesus' disciples because of social pressures.
"Nevertheless many even of the authorities believed in him, but
for fear of the Pharisees they did not confess it, lest they should
be put out of the synagogue: for they loved the praise of men
more than the praise of God" (John 12:42-43, RSV). Note the
phrase, "They loved the praise of men more than the praise of
God." We all need the affirmation of other people. At every stage
of life we crave the approval of our peers. It appears that some
would sell their soul for the intoxicating praise of others.

Note that the Gospel writer speaks of the "praise of God."

Imagine, having the approval of our Creator! The Lord's affirmation comes to his disciples, not simply at their death or in the day of judgment, but here and now, as well. We are tempted to settle for lesser loyalties and more immediate rewards, but no affirmation could be lovelier than the approval of God.

When we believe, we become Jesus' disciples and he saves us from the tyranny of sin. He changes our life for *good*.

Christ is calling still—to be with him, and to be sent forth to share the faith. "Follow me and I will make you become fishers of men" (Mark 1:17, RSV). That was not simply an ancient invitation issued beside the Sea of Galilee. It is also the risen Christ's current imperative for all who would be his disciples. He calls us out of the darkness of sin into the light of his marvelous grace.

You don't have to believe—but you may! Discipleship is what you do, after you say, "I believe."

A Prayer:

Dear Father, we pray in gratitude for your grace in calling us to become your disciples. We are unworthy of such a high compliment, but we shall be thankful for it all our lives. We are grateful you take the initiative in calling us to faith, and then give us hearts to respond. Make us your devoted and courageous disciples.

Forgive, we pray, those things we have done and thought which displease you, as well as the right we have failed to do.

We pray for all who carry heavy burdens of illness, sorrow, hard decisions, or doubts. Strengthen and heal them—and give to us the ministry of encouragement; that we may help them, as well.

Father, we thank you for your church—the family of God. Grant us spiritual revival that we may be renewed and that new disciples may be called to believe. Bless our missionary outreach, our worship, and our love. May we thrill at the cry of newborn babes in Christ, as they come professing their faith.

We pray that you will continue calling those who are to become your disciples. Help us continually to adjust our vision that we may see you more clearly and be your faithful followers, through Jesus Christ our Lord. Amen.

6
Discipleship as Discipline

Matthew 7:13-14

These familiar verses of our text read like this in Clarence Jordan's *Cotton Patch Version:* "Approach life through the gate of discipline, for the way that leads to emptiness is wide and easy, and a lot of folks are taking that approach. But the gate into the full life is hard, and the road is bumpy, and only a few take this route" (Matt. 7:13-14).

Life has a way of coming to the crossroads, of calling for a decision. This is surely part of what it means to be made in the image of God; the ability to make a choice, to decide. Indeed, indecision can be a type of hell. The psychologist talks about "choice anxiety." In order to say yes to certain persons and things, we must say no to others. A man has to leave his parents if he is to cleave to his wife. Perhaps you heard about the lady whose counselor asked, "Do you have trouble making up your mind?" She replied, "Well, yes and no."

Persons in the Bible were constantly facing important decisions. Abraham had to decide whether he would follow God's invitation to pilgrimage. Moses said to his contemporaries, "I have set before you this day life . . . and death. . . . Therefore, choose life" (Deut. 30:15,19, RSV). Joshua was to echo Moses a generation later by issuing this challenge: "Choose you this day whom ye will serve" (Josh. 24:15, KJV). Jesus was also throwing down a gauntlet by inviting his generation to forsake the wide gate and broad way for the narrow gate and way which leads to life. The poet, John Oxenham, issued a similar call with his verse:

> To every man there openeth
> A way and ways and a way
> And the high soul treads the high way,
> And the low soul gropes the low;
> And in between on the misty flats
> The rest drift to and fro;
> But to every man there openeth
> A high way and a low;
> And every man decideth
> The way his soul shall go.

The Christian way is the way of discipline. We are aware that discipline is an unpopular word in our time. Yet, without it, little is accomplished in any realm. Who would want to be operated on by a surgeon who lacked the discipline to master his profession? The musician pays the price of practice in order to play well. Every successful athlete must be a disciplined player. Bird hunters who shoot at a covey often fail to get a bird. But those who aim at a single bird usually bring home meat. Contractors have to follow the discipline of the architect's plan. A successful marriage involves forsaking others and belonging to one person, "so long as you both shall live." It may sound narrow, but that is essential to a happy marriage.

The undisciplined life is hardly worth living. If discipleship is what we do after we believe, then discipline is the way to successful discipleship. The truth is, the undisciplined person is not so free as he thinks. The broad way is easy and crowded, but those who travel it are really slaves—to comfort and selfishness. Someone said of a river—it follows the way of least resistance and that's why it's so crooked! A river out of its channel may cause a destructive flood, or it may simply become a swamp filled with frogs and wiggletails. The undisciplined way requires little effort and has few rewards. While we are open to new truth, it is possible to be too open-minded, too intellectually hospitable. All truth is tested against Christ who is Truth. The author of Hebrews wrote about "a new and living way" (10:20). Christ pioneered this way, and we follow him. What we need as Christians is not lower goals but strength to achieve the goals to which Jesus calls us. We dare not remain on the misty flats of indecision.

The Discipline of the Yoke of Christ

The gospel is invitation—to believe and to serve. As the cross represents what Christ has done for us, so the yoke represents what we do for Christ, or our Christian service. E. Hermond Westmoreland tells about a visit to the church of Notre Dame in Copenhagen. It was a cold December day. Ice and snow covered the ground outside as he entered the dimly-lit cathedral. Walking down the center aisle, he noted the statues of the apostles. Judas' place had been taken by Paul.

Dr. Westmoreland knelt at the altar and looked up at the towering statue of Christ by Thorvaldsen. He noted the eyes of the statue and the hands extended in invitation. Dr. Westmoreland said, "I did not have to know Danish to understand the inscription in gold at the base of the statue. It meant, 'Come unto me.'"

1. *The Invitation:* "Come to me, all who labor and are heavy laden, and I will give you rest" (Matt. 11:28, RSV).

It is a simple invitation. There is no long list saying we are to do this or not do that. We are not required by Christ to believe a given body of doctrine or dogma. We are not told to dress in a certain way or even to have a particular life-style. The invitation is simply, "Come to me; follow me; believe me."

> Just as I am, poor, wretched, blind;
>   Sight, riches, healing of the mind,
> Yea, all I need in Thee to find,
>   O Lamb of God, I come! I come!

It is a *personal* invitation, "Come to me." Imagine these words on the lips of any contemporary statesman. They would be ludicrous. Only Jesus, the incarnate Son of God could issue such an invitation.

It is also a personal invitation in that we must respond to it personally. No one else can make that decision for us—not our wife, mother, or friend.

Notice who is invited to follow Christ: "*All* who labor and are heavy laden." This means all working men and women. It means more: all who are burdened. Jesus' original hearers were carrying a burdensome religion. It was legalistic and cold. Their religion consisted of a collection of rules and prohibitions. For many it was a religion to be borne, instead of one which would bear them up. Jesus wants to deliver us from a burdensome religion and give us the lighter yoke of love.

Jesus also invited all who are anxious and fearful to come to him. This characteristic cuts across all groupings. Youth are anxious about their education, getting a job, being successful in love. Singles are pressured by parents, to "marry and give us grandchildren!" Young adults are working to get established and to rear their children. They are plagued by "too much month at the end of the money." Middle age has its pressures and anxieties, to care for the young and the old. What if an accident or major medical crisis should come to middle adults? The elderly face an unknown and sometimes frightening future. Many of these folk have more friends on the other side of death than on this side. "Come to me," said Jesus, "my peace I give to you." "Come to me," said Jesus, "and I will give you rest." This rest is not necessarily idleness. It could be better translated renewal or refreshment. His invitation gives us encouragement and hope.

2. *The Offer:* "Take my yoke . . . and learn from me."

Discipline is not popular. The current mind-set is expressed in Whitman's poem.

> I'm as free as a breeze
>   What's to stop me and why
> I can live as I please
>   Open road, open sky.

Yet, the truth is: Every man has a yoke of some kind. It may be your selfish pride. You will not give yourself to anyone—will not love anyone. Then don't be surprised to discover that no one loves you. What a heavy yoke!

Your yoke may be your freedom itself. You want to be free, man! You want to do your own thing and answer to no one. So you go from beer to bourbon, from "pot" to "horse"—only to discover that life is a big bore. Pleasure alone never satisfies. Your very liberty can become a slave's chain.

Your sin and guilt can be a heavy, galling yoke. It hurts you, others, and God. Saul Kane said, "He made me see the harm I had done by being me."

Christ issues an invitation to exchange yokes. "Come to me, learn of me, be my disciple, learn my discipline—take my yoke." Notice that the yoke of Christ is taken voluntarily. No man is saved against his will. Take the yoke of Christ. It is the yoke of faith—believe in Christ. It is the yoke of discipleship—follow Christ. It is the yoke of love—love Christ and your fellowmen.

The late C. Roy Angell of Florida was a great storyteller. I understand that his wife tried to stop his telling stories in the pulpit. Fortunately for us, she was no more successful at influencing her husband than most wives are. Dr. Angell told a story that illustrates the beauty of a voluntary discipline:[1]

Out West there lived a little, bow-legged cowboy. He had reared a colt, and it had grown to be a big fine stallion. He and the horse loved each other very much. Everybody teased the little cowboy about his horse. It would follow him around like a dog. The horse had stepped in a gopher hole and sprained its ankle and had been put out in the big pasture. Some wild horses had broken in and then broken out again, and the favorite stallion had gone with them. The cowboy was just miserable.

One evening one of the hands raced into the ranch as hard as his horse could run, yelling to the dejected little cowboy at the top of his voice: "Found your horse! Found your horse! He's with a herd of wild horses not far from here, down in the canyon."

It was late in the evening, and the little cowboy got set to go after his horse before daylight the next morning. He climbed up on top of the rimrock where he could look down the long canyon. There were the horses grazing quietly. The little cowboy went down on foot. He did a beautiful piece of stalking until he was close enough for his voice to reach his horse. Then he stood up, and all of those horses were suddenly on the alert, their heads up. He was talking to his horse for all he was worth. Then the herd bolted—all but one. One of them stood still, but he didn't know what to do. He looked at the other horses, and he took a step or two; then he looked back at the cowboy, pranced around a little, then looked again.

The cross-pull in that fine stallion must have been terrible. There was the master whom he had loved, and there was the wild herd with which he had run. Which way should he go? For a moment it looked as though the cowboy had lost, for the horse took half a dozen steps toward the herd, which was galloping away in a cloud of dust. Then he stopped and looked back, and with his head up and neck arched, he trotted to his master. The cowboy put a rope around his neck, petted and caressed him, and cried a little, too. The horse nuzzled his pockets, and the cowboy reached into one of them and brought out a handfull of lump sugar.

There is a discipline and yoke which we take voluntarily and joyfully.

3. *The Promise:* "My yoke is easy, and my burden is light."

This sounds like a paradox—and it is. What Jesus meant was, "My yoke fits well, thus making the load light." An old commentator said his yoke is "lined with love." Jesus was a carpenter and knew that yokes must be tailor-made to fit well.

You have a gift, an ability, a talent. God has a task for you; a work for you to do. Find his will for your life (his yoke) and give God your best. Some discover the will of God for their lives easily. For others, it comes harder. In seeking his will follow the gleam that comes in your prayer and devotional life. Consider your gifts and talents. How can these be developed and used to help others and glorify God? You will also want to consult with more mature disciples to learn how God led them and how they see you might best serve him. You will discover his yoke is not a burden, but a blessing.

The yoke of Christ is always *a double yoke.* Christ wears it with you! You are never alone. Christ is your yokefellow and "we are labourers together with God" (1 Cor. 3:9, KJV).

Can you join with Horatius Bonar, the hymn writer, in his concern.

> I heard the voice of Jesus say,
>   "Come unto Me and rest;
> Lay down, thou weary one, lay down
>   Thy head upon my breast."

Perhaps you have already responded in his words.

> I came to Jesus as I was,
>   Weary and worn and sad;
> I found in Him a resting-place,
>   And He has made me glad.

7
Discipleship and the Devotional Life

Christian, are you anemic? You may be suffering due to a deficient spiritual diet. What distinguishes you from your pagan neighbors? Is there a discernable difference in your life-style and theirs? Someone said it has become almost impossible to tell the sheep from the goats! I hope all believers would agree that we need an enriched devotional life. A rich, growing devotional life, which includes both private and corporate worship, will make us healthy disciples of the Lord Christ.

An estimated fifty million Americans go to church on any given Sunday. While they go for a variety of reasons, their basic intent is to join in corporate worship. The word *worship* comes from an Anglo-Saxon word, *worthship*. It means to ascribe supreme worth to God. The psalmist gave expression to this idea when he wrote, "Give unto the Lord the glory due unto his name" (29:2). Christian worship took its basic pattern from the synagogue service which featured the reading and interpretation of Scripture, and prayer. Christians added the celebration of the Lord's Supper, baptism, and an expansion of congregational singing. Many hymns of early Christian worship are found in the New Testament.

Our worship has two basic functions: comfort and confrontation.

"Comfort ye, comfort ye my people, saith your God" (Isa. 40:1, KJV). We find comfort in the service—in the pastoral prayer and often in the music, Scripture reading, and sermon. A British theologian said, "I don't give tuppence (two cents) for the man who tells me where my duty lies, but I'll give all to the man who tells me whence my help comes."

A second, and equally valuable function of worship is to confront the worshiper with the claims of the gospel and the demands of the Christian ethic. True worship presents both demand and promise, judgment, and love.

Worship also calls for our commitment, our response. The test of our worship is our changed lives in the world. True worship results in a growing devotion to God, and a growing sensitivity to the needs of others. We seek to have the mind of Christ, to see with his eyes, and feel with his compassion. Worship results in our encounter with God. This does not occur in every worship service or in every time of personal devotion. However, it *does* occur, and we are never quite the same afterwards. To worship is to experience the presence of God, realize our sinfulness, sincerely repent, and dedicate ourselves anew to his service.

Soren Kierkegaard, the Danish theologian, described worship in an interesting way. He said it is like a play in which the worshipers are actors, the prompter is the preacher and worship leader, and the audience is God. In this view, our worship is our sacrifice or our offering to God.

Our worship is a never-ending, never-completed experience. Harry Emerson Fosdick had a summer home on the Maine Coast. He said that each time he went there he fell in love with the sea all over again. He wrote, "I do not know all the sea: where the Amazon empties, where lie Antarctica's frozen wastes, or where the warm Pacific washes tropical island beaches. Yet, I know the sea near me! I do not know all of God, yet I know something of him. Believe in as much of God as you can. That is the way to start." Our worship involves encountering God, ascribing supreme worth to him, being comforted by his person, and confronted by his gospel. Only man worships, and only man celebrates the good news of God.

Another aspect of the Christian's devotional life is prayer. We pray in response to God's invitation to his disciples: "Call to me and I will answer you, and tell you great things which you have not known" (Jer. 33:3, RSV). Jesus' disciples asked Jesus to teach them only one thing—how to pray! This seems strange when as good Jews, they already prayed three times each day. They must have sensed something more in their Master's prayer life than the routine. Jesus' prayer life was not shallow form or meaningless ritual. It had a force, a power which really communicated with the Father. You cannot understand the might of the Nile river without knowing the high mountains and torrential rains in the heart of Africa which feed it. Neither can you understand the person and teachings of Jesus apart from his rich prayer life.

Glenn Hinson has given us a simple outline which helps us understand the place of prayer in the disciple's devotional life. He suggests that prayer is turning on, turning in, and turning over.[1]

Prayer is communication with God, and it begins with our turning on to God's presence all round us. We believe that God is present in the world he created (though he is far more than "Father Nature"). God is also present in and comes to us through other people, both great and small. God will speak through our conscience or inner person, if we listen. As Christ's disciples we believe that God's supreme self-revelation was in the person and work of Jesus. We encounter Jesus in the Scriptures and in the Person of the Holy Spirit who is the Spirit of Jesus.

Turning on to God means learning to pray expectantly. We

close our eyes and bow our heads when we pray. Many Christians also kneel. These postures of prayer date from the Middle Ages. They reflect an attitude of concentration (closing out the world by closing our eyes) and subservience (bowing and kneeling). Interestingly, the attitude of prayer by Jesus' contemporaries was to stand, open-eyed, lifting one's hands toward heaven, palms up. This attitude was one of expectation: to receive a blessing from the Lord. Think of it, in prayer we talk with the Creator who is also our heavenly Father! Prayer is turning on to God's presence.

And prayer is turning in. It includes listening for a word from God: meditation. Prayer involves waiting for God's leading, his direction, his impressions for our daily life.

I've found it helpful to think of God with my first waking moment. As you wake up, recite some familiar verse such as, "This is the day which the Lord has made; let us rejoice and be glad in it," or "Great is the Lord and greatly to be praised" (Pss. 118:24; 48:1, RSV). This initial thought of the day can set the tone for the rest of it.

Most disciples find a need for a quiet time sometime during the day. This may be a stated time early in the day, at noon, or in the evening with the family. One friend finds brief moments throughout the day in which he kicks his work load into neutral and "centers down" on the spiritual life. Most of us need a definite time for personal devotions. A business executive has a time alone in his office just after lunch. His secretary reports that the boss is "in consultation" during this time. He sits and reads the Scripture, thinks about it and its application, spends some time in prayer, and makes notes of his impressions. He finds this a helpful discipline.

Prayer as turning in includes self-examination and confession. It includes more. It centers on God's adequacy, might, and knowledge. It acknowledges him as our Shepherd as well as ourselves as his sheep. Prayer lays hold of God's strength for our weakness, his courage for our fears, healing for our hurt, and hope for our despair. Turning in through prayer lets God's Holy Spirit lay hold of us and lift us up to unimagined heights.

J. Clyde Turner described God's grace and man's anxiety vividly. He said we are like a mouse in the granaries of Egypt after the seven years of plenty; afraid we'll eat all the grain and starve. Father Joseph says, "Eat on, little mouse, my granaries are sufficient for thee." Or we are like a fish in the mighty Mississippi River, afraid we'll drink all its water and die in the sun. Old Man River says, "Drink on, little fish, my waters are sufficient for thee." Or, we are like a man standing on a mountaintop, fearful of breathing up all the oxygen and suffocating. God says, "Breathe on, little man, my atmosphere is sufficient for thee." So God says to his weary disciples, "Pray on, work on, live on, my grace is sufficient for thee."

Prayer is also turning over, our surrender to the lordship of Christ. This can be difficult and costly. I recall vividly my call to the gospel ministry—and my resistance to the call. I had other goals and ambitions. What the struggle came down to in the final analysis was whether I was willing to let Christ be Lord of my life, as well as Savior. In prayer, as surrender, we learn to let Christ be Lord.

Be careful what you desire; for desire is a form of prayer. What you really desire you often get. There is a terrifying text in the Psalms: "He gave them their request; but sent leanness into their soul" (106:15, KJV). Careful how you pray! Prayer's supreme answer is a gift—God gives himself to those who sincerely pray. Prayer is as large as life. Obviously, our discussion of prayer in the disciple's devotional life also applies to his systematic reading and study of the Scriptures. Our devotional life includes both public and private worship, prayer, and Bible study. The risen

Christ's invitation to devotion and service is found in Revelation 3:20: "Behold, I stand at the door, and knock: if any man hear my voice, and open the door, I will come in."

Studdert-Kennedy expressed man's dual nature in a poem:

> I'm a man and a man's a mixture,
> Right down from his very birth,
> For part of him comes from heaven,
> And part of him comes from earth.

This reflects the Genesis account which tells us that man was made in the image of God and from the dust of the earth. Dale Moody expresses this truth by saying man is kin to God and kin to the clod. He is both a creature and a spiritual being. Prayer gives expression to man's vertical nature.

Prayer is not a monologue—it includes both speaking with God and listening to him. It is not magic, a way of getting the Almighty to be our genie in a jug. Neither is prayer—mouching—trying to get God to be a laborsaving device. God will not do for us what we can very well do for ourselves.

Prayer is communication with God, both verbal and nonverbal. It is approaching God boldly, with confidence in our Father, yet not with undue familiarity. Prayer is really conformity of our will with his. In Romans we are told not to be conformed to the world (12:2).

J. B. Phillips paraphrases that verse, "Don't let the world around you squeeze you into its own mold." That reminds me of my Grandmother's butter mold, which invariably left the pattern of an acorn on top of the butter. Paul also told us in Romans, "Be conformed to the image of his Son" (8:29). Prayer helps bring us into line with the divine will and purpose. Little wonder it is an essential in the disciple's devotional life.

Prayer takes many forms: adoration and praise, confession of sin, gratitude and thanksgiving, and intercession—the most unselfish kind of prayer. In our prayer life we should strive to pray not so much "give me" as "make me." A Scottish writer reminds us that the most common prayer of all is, "God, my will be done." But the greatest prayer is, "Thy will be done."

The cultivation of our devotional life as Jesus' disciples calls for both meditation and Christian service. It requires a simplification of life in which we clear our schedule in order to have time for what is of primary importance. The devotional life also calls for seeing persons as being of first value and things as secondary. Our time calls for the development of an ecological conscience to use things wisely and well.

The conflict between devotional religion and practical religion is illustrated in an account from Luke 10:38-42. The household in the small village was all abuzz because the preacher was coming for dinner. He was no ordinary guest, but Jesus of Nazareth! (Imagine having Jesus for your dinner guest!) Martha was the practical Jane. She barked orders right and left. She probably sent her brother, Lazarus, to the market for some last-minute items. Her sister, Mary, was making the dust fly (after all, it hadn't rained for four months, and there was plenty of dust). Martha was a blurr of activity.

Wouldn't you know it, Jesus arrived earlier than expected! In the kitchen, Martha was in a frenzy. A puff of wind had blown the fire out and it had to be remade. The yeast bread wouldn't rise, and the butter wouldn't come in the hanging goat-skin churn. To top everything else, the cheese was molded beyond use! And Mary, where was Mary? There she was in the front room, sitting at Jesus' feet: listening to him like a man. Didn't she know her place was in the kitchen? Martha blurted out her criticism. "Would the Master please send Mary to the kitchen to help?" she asked. Jesus gave Martha a mild rebuke, pointing out that Mary had chosen the more important thing. What a cameo from the daily life of Jesus and his friends, and how true to life today!

Jesus is Lord of the pots and pans. Practical Martha was an activist, a dynamo, perhaps a workaholic. She served God with her hands, in the midst of her ordinary tasks. And, there is truth here. But service divorced from worship has little value. It may simply be busy work, without spiritual content. It is true that we can give a cup of cold water in Jesus' name, but we must also give more. We must share our faith with others as well.

Jesus is *Lord* of the quiet hour. Mary was a pietist, a quiet, contemplative type. She could listen to Jesus by the hour, drinking in his teachings. Perhaps Mary was sensitive to some deep need in Jesus' life just at that juncture. Jesus was within the shadow of the cross. Perhaps having a sympathetic listener at that point was a great help to him. Certainly we know Mary needed the bread of heaven that Jesus was sharing. Mary gave priority to spiritual bread.

Obviously, we need both solitude and service, inspiration and perspiration, spirituality and actuality. We need both the hands of Martha and the heart of Mary. It is important to keep them in the right order; to know when to give attention to which one.

Our devotional life as Christ's disciples calls for our giving attention to worship, both private and corporate—with the people of God. It requires the growth of a rich prayer life and consistent study of the Scriptures. And it demands a balance of both practical Christian service and withdrawal for spiritual renewal. We come in to worship and go out to serve.

A Prayer:

Father, we come in adoration and praise.

You are our Creator—we owe life itself to you.

You are our Sustainer—we owe all to your providential care.

Thank you, Father, that you care.

"A God who doesn't care, doesn't count."
You are our patient, loving Father.
May every heart thrill with your praise!

Father, we confess our sins to you.
We are away from you
without ever leaving the premises.
We are selfish and ingrown,
proud and self-sufficient,
callous and uncaring.
O Lord, forgive. . . . Thank you!

Father, we thank you
That you forgive our sins,
That you provide our needs,
That you are present with us even now.
Thank you for this worshiping, serving congregation—the people of
God.
Thank you for this free land
and our democratic government.
Make us good citizens.

Father, we pray for others—
for those who govern us—guide them;
for those who went before us—make us grateful;
for those who follow us—make them wise.

God grant us the dedicated hands of Martha,
and the dedicated heart of Mary.

Bless all who need your grace just now.
those who suffer pain, bereavement, doubt,
those who face hard decisions;
Make us adequate, for the living of these days.
Through Jesus Christ, our Lord. Amen.

8
Discipleship as Ministry

Salvation is free but discipleship is costly! You cannot earn or buy salvation. It can only be rejected or accepted as a gift. But discipleship is costly! Jesus reminded his disciples to count the cost before glibly saying they would follow him anywhere. Salvation involves the whole person and is a total event embracing our past, present, and future. To be Christ's disciple involves a personal ministry with personal costs.

Dietrich Bonhoeffer, a German theologian, accused the church of preaching "cheap grace." He said the church is guilty of offering forgiveness without requiring repentance; it offers grace without requiring discipleship. Bonhoeffer added: "When Christ calls a man, he calls him to come and die." That cost may be literal as it was in Bonhoeffer's case. (He was hanged by the Nazis in 1945.) Following Christ will always cost our will, as we surrender to do his. Discipleship calls on us to pay the price; to be growing persons—in our love, our service, our understanding, and our compassion. Discipleship calls for giving Christ first place: priority!

Discipleship means that every Christian has a ministry, through the church and personally. Both types of ministry are necessary.

Let us consider:

Our Ministry Through the Church

The church is under fire both from without and from within. This is nothing new! One leading churchman accused the church of some serious gaps. He said we are guilty of a *credibility* gap. The church preaches doctrines which many of its members do not believe. One survey indicated that in one main-line denomination only 24 percent of its members believed in the second coming of Christ. But since when did popular opinion determine the validity of religious truth?

This leader also accused the church of a *relevance* gap. He said the church is shut up within its own walls, insulated from the real issues of life, and is as silent as a tomb on these issues. It is true that the church can become ingrown and insensitive to the hurts of those outside our doors. The church can be guilty of simply perpetuating the *status quo*—"lowering our voices to raise our budgets." However, the church in many places has both a prophetic voice and a social conscience!

Our friend further said that the church is guilty of a *performance* gap. He said that the more persons become involved in church the less ethical they become in their behavior. These are terrible charges from a brilliant critic. We must admit that they contain a germ of truth, though we would like to deny their basic validity.

The church can best answer its critics by fulfilling its New Testament pattern. Many metaphors describe the nature of the church and the Christian disciples' ministry through it.

Christians are called "a chosen race." This speaks of God's initiative in calling us to faith. We are called a "royal priesthood." Every believer is a priest before God. This means we have direct access to God, without having to go through any mediator except Christ. It also means that we are persons for others, that we are responsible to share our faith. Disciples are also called a "holy nation"—we are dedicated to God, set apart for his ministry and service. We are "God's own people," his personal possession. Now we belong to Jesus! (See 1 Pet. 2:1-10.)

One of the most vivid metaphors used in the New Testament to describe the church is "God's building" in which we are "living stones." "You as living stones are being built into a spiritual house." (See Eph. 2:19-20; 1 Pet. 2:5.)

As disciples, we are God's building material (v. 19). Before we were converted, we were strangers to the covenant of promise. As Gentiles, we were not God's chosen people and had no rights or claim on any special relationship with him. We were like foreigners in a strange land. We did not belong to God. We were lost in the darkness and loneliness of sin unforgiven.

Our present status in Christ is vastly different. As Jesus' disciples we are "fellow citizens" of the colony of heaven on earth, the church. This means we have a dual citizenship: on earth and in heaven. As believers in Christ, we are now members of the family of God. We belong! We are children of the King, sons and heirs of immortality.

Disciples make up the church which is God's building (v. 20). The building's foundations are the prophets or inspired preachers of the Old Testament, and the apostles who were eyewitnesses to the Christ-event. We might add to the prophets and apostles our spiritual forebearers in the church's history. We owe a great debt to early Christians, the reformers, and those who brought the faith to our land, converting our ancestors. We are the heirs of their vision and sacrifice. It is part of our stewardship to honor their finest traditions and to pass them on to the succeeding generation.

Christ himself is the chief cornerstone of God's building, the church. Using today's terminology, we might call Christ the church's steel superstructure. Man alone cannot build the church; God does that. And man cannot destroy the church. We can only fail it. Where Christ is, there is the church.

The church is a growing, unfinished building (v. 21). The church is built not of brick and concrete, but of flesh and blood—"living stones." A bellows breathes but it is not alive. A church is more than an organization. It is an organism—growing, changing, never static. The church of Jesus Christ is in the process of being built. It is not yet complete. As an illustration of the incompleteness of the spiritual church, consider the construction of a church building. The Washington Cathedral in our nation's capital was suggested by George Washington nearly 200 years ago. Construction was begun seventy years ago, and it will not be complete until 1991! It is taking three generations to build the cathedral (and $30,000,000). Only God knows how many centuries it will require to complete the living church, which is his body. It is incomplete so long as there are others to be won to faith in Christ.

The living church, made up of all Christ's disciples, is a glorious building (v. 22). It is to be "a dwelling place for God." The ancients had a tabernacle made of animal skins. Solomon's temple in Jerusalem was built of stone. The church, God's building today, is made of flesh-and-blood disciples who are empowered by his Spirit. Without a soul a body is a corpse, and without the Holy Spirit the church is also dead. May the beauty of our devotion and the faithfulness of our daily lives become a lovely sanctuary for the "dwelling place of God."

The Bible describes Christ as the "chief corner stone" of those who believe and follow him. However, it also calls Christ the "stone of stumbling" for those who reject him. This vividly points up the necessity of faith and for building our lives on him. Our relationship to Jesus determines whether we have life or destruction.

Many of us find our ministry given expression through the church. We cherish its worship and are nourished by its teaching of the Scriptures. However, the test of our faith is not simply what happens while we are at church—caught up in its worship and praise, sharing, and fellowship. The real test is what happens after we leave the church—at home and school, at work, and at the club. This points to:

Our Ministry Within

Disciples withdraw from the world for private worship. This principle of withdrawal is essential. The world is too much with us. You can't escape its noise and selling or even its entertainment. Music surrounds us—in the dentist's chair, in elevators, the supermarket, and restaurants. It's hard to be quiet. We may even be afraid of the "sound of silence."

Jesus is our example in withdrawal. He was present in public worship services, and he often left clamouring human need to spend time quietly with his disciples or alone with his heavenly Father. Elton Trueblood says that if you are always available to everyone, you are not worth much when you are available. If Jesus needed retreat, withdrawal, silence, and prayer—how much more do we? Times of spiritual renewal and refueling are essential if we are to live effective Christian lives in the world.

However, there are dangers in the contemplative life-style. One is that we may be tempted to compartmentalize life, to separate our religious life from our daily life in the business world and home. Such separation develops a kind of spiritual split personality which is hypocritical.

A second danger in placing an overemphasis on the principle of withdrawal is that we can become ingrown. We may emphasize the other world until we are of little earthly good. There is a temptation to become modern monastics. Nothing could be further from the mind of Christ who said his disciples are to be "in the world but not of the world."

The church withdrawn is to be balanced by the church militant, involved, serving in the world. The original disciples were told to go into all the world, and "as you go, evangelize."

One of the most exciting things happening in the Christian church currently is the recovery of the personal ministry of the laity, the people of God. Every believer has a call to this kind of ministry. All disciples are expected to be ministers of Jesus Christ, where they are. We are all to seek to win others to faith in Christ and to have a personal ministry of encouragement.

Our Ministry Without!

As the people of God we are a gathered community—called together by God to hear a word from beyond. But we are also to be a scattered community—sent out from formal worship and private meditation to apply the gospel in our daily living. Nothing less will honor our Lord and nothing else will capture the imagination of our times!

Once a man arrived late at church. The people were already going home. He asked an usher, "Is the service over?" The wise usher replied, "The worship is over, but the service is just beginning."

You may ask—"But what do I do? I don't have time for organized visitation or the date set for an evangelistic outreach doesn't fit my schedule. Therefore, I can't participate."

But, this is the day of "doing your own thing" and in what better way can you do this than through Christian service? Begin in an area that we all share:

Christian citizenship. Have I registered to vote? If I have moved recently, have I informed the voter registration office? Am I informed on the issues and on the qualifications of the candidates—local, state, and national? Do I have qualifications needed to assure *good* government but don't I think I can afford to get into the field—it's too dirty and too expensive! Did I help get other persons registered or can I help on election day to get persons to the polls? Or, if *you* really believe in a candidate, you can address envelopes, write personal notes on his behalf, or distribute literature on your block.

You can continue good citizenship by paying taxes, keeping up with vital issues, writing to congressmen when they do a good job—not just when they "goof!" We are exhorted by Jesus "to pray for those in authority over us."

There are elderly people you could adopt. Person-to-person encounters can be so meaningful both ways. Nursing homes and homes for the aged will be glad to provide names. Often, these persons are not in financial need or physically impaired—they just want a friend who'll visit and listen and share. A trip to the grocery, drug store, or park will make the whole week happier for them and for you! A group of beauticians offer a half day in one home to shampoo and set hair for elderly ladies.

Transportation can be provided for congregate feeding or craft and recreation classes held at churches or other community facilities. Ladies from several churches in many cities and towns aid in delivering "Mobile Meals" to persons unable to travel.

Have you thought how much *good* you can do through the civic organizations you belong to? Many have programs to sponsor youth groups so that they can be trained in community leadership for the future. Others provide scholarships for worthy students or furnish clothing, food, and friendship for international students. Scouting, Boys' Clubs, Blue Birds, the "Y", Key Clubs, Junior Civitans, Young Rotarians are only a few of the groups available.

Our schools provide opportunities to meet needs. You may find ways of helping a child through tutoring, or avenues of meeting physical needs such as helping provide breakfast for hungry children at the school. Being a friend to a fatherless child or a motherless teenager can be a great help.

The disciple can find many opportunities for personal ministry in the world. What are your gifts and how can you use them to help others? Talents in music and drama can be put to good use, as well as hobbies.

If Christ's disciple is sensitive to the Spirit's leading, he can find a point of contact with unsaved persons, and share his faith. All of us know persons who need the Lord. We can win their confidence and tell them what Christ means in our experience. When the opportunity comes, we can then share the way of salvation.

Disciples are God's people on mission. We are to "shew forth the praises of him who hath called you out of darkness into his marvelous light" (1 Pet. 2:9, KJV). Eugene O'Neill wrote about a family's disintegration in a story entitled, *Long Day's Journey into Night*. For the disciple, life becomes a "long day's journey into light." We are on mission for the Master—across the world and across the street. William R. Merrill phrased the challenge in these words:

> Rise up, O men of God!
>   Have done with lesser things;
> Give heart and mind and soul and strength
>   To serve the King of kings.

A famous American churchman said that a God who does not care does not count. The same may be said of a disciple or of the church. Ours is a caring ministry, atune to human needs. May we become the company of the caring! Effective discipleship calls for both meaningful worship and dedicated service to others.

A Prayer:

Father, we are grateful that your Son has shown us that you

care for us. We respond in love to you and to others for whom Christ died.

We pray that our worship will be worthy and our faith attractive to those without. Grant that we will bear a faithful witness to you and encourage others by our ministry.

Heighten our sense of mission, that we may think less of our achievements and more of your grace. May we be obedient to your will and be empowered by your Holy Spirit.

We dedicate ourselves and our resources to our personal ministry within the church and beyond. May we be part of something larger than we are, and larger than our local church. Through our support of missions, extend our ministry across the earth. Through Jesus Christ, our Lord. Amen.

9
John, Son of Thunder

A Dramatic Monologue

Wouldn't you like to have known the apostles in person? Suppose you could go back to the year A.D. 96. You are at the home of Alexander, the Greek pastor of the church in Ephesus, in Asia Minor. You are listening to the aged apostle John as he talks with Alexander. The two men, one not thirty and the other past ninety, are sitting in an open courtyard. There are lovely spring flowers all about and the air is filled with their fragrance and the sound of birds singing. The two sit soaking up the warm morning sun. Listen as John speaks, haltingly at first and then more clearly as he warms to his narration.

"Alexander, my young brother, you have been so kind to me. You and your dear people practice the Christian virtue of hospitality most graciously. I am in your debt. You've taken this old man in as though I were your father. Indeed, I do feel a fatherly affection for you and your congregation. They have been kind to me. They say I appear twenty years younger than I am. Age is a strange thing. It becomes the old man's badge of distinction. Suddenly, we don't feel complimented when we are taken to be younger than we are. I suppose that's all part of our human vanity. But here I am chattering about nonessentials when I want to take this morning with you to tell you some important visions I haven't discussed with anyone yet. I want to tell you what a difference Jesus has made in my life, and I want you to understand my divine compulsion to share the most encouraging words Christians can read today. I also want you to understand what I've recently experienced, and to commit it to writing so the churches can circulate copies and read it in their assemblies. The churches here in Asia, and beyond, must hear the risen Christ's message.

"My recent exile on Patmos in the Agean Sea was no friend to age. The constant dampness and my meager living conditions in that island cave took their toll on my health. It has grown fragile, I fear. When Emperor Domitian was murdered last fall, the Senate in Rome repealed his oppressive laws and freed all political prisoners. You can't imagine the ecstatic joy I felt at my release.

"I shall always recall with joy your congregation's grand welcome. They were so excited at my release. They made my homecoming a thing of beauty. I recall that they packed out the meeting place here in your courtyard. I was so weak from my ordeal that I had to be helped into the meeting by two of your deacons, Rufus and Tychicus. Tychicus is the brother who brought the letter from Missionary Paul to Ephesus. Though you were away at the time, you have every reason to feel a pastor's pride in your people. I was so weak that I could not preach. While the men supported me, I kept saying to your dear people, 'Little children, love one another. Little children, love one another.'

"The privation on Patmos was not the worst of it, Alexander. The hardest thing was the separation. To be called to preach the good news and then be shut away from people is torture. One of the glorious things I saw in my vision of the Holy City is that there is no more sea there—no more separation! Indeed, that will be glory! We will be with him, and with our beloved who are in Christ. But more about that later.

"My, that warm goat's milk was good! That, added to this sun, will warm these old bones inside and out. Helen is a fine cook. You were fortunate in many ways in the happy choice of a wife. No one is more important in a man's ministry than his companion of the way. Excuse me, I'm rambling again.

"To come to the point, Alexander, while I was on Patmos I had a number of visions. I've come to see what the last days will be like, and I've heard a series of messages from the risen Christ to the churches of the Province of Asia. In a vision on the Lord's Day I heard a voice which said, 'I am Alpha and Omega, who is and who was, and who is coming, the Almighty.' Then I heard the voice behind me loud as a trumpet-call command me to write down in a book what I saw and to send it to the seven churches—to Ephesus, Smyrna, Pergamum, Thyatira, Sardis, Philadelphia, and Laodicea.

"I turned to see who was speaking to me, and I saw seven golden lampstands. Among them I saw someone like the Son of man. He was dressed in a long robe with a golden belt around his waist, his hair was snow-white, his eyes blazed like fire, and his feet shone as the finest bronze glows in the furnace. His voice sounded like the roar of a great waterfall. In his right hand he held seven stars. A sharp two-edged sword came out of his mouth, and his face was shining like the sun at its height. When my eyes took in this sight, I fell at his feet. He placed his right hand on me and said,

" 'Do not be afraid. I am the first and the last, the Living One. I am he who was dead, and now you see me alive for endless ages! I hold in my hand the keys of death and the grave. I am victor over them. Therefore, write what you have seen, both the things which are now, and the things which are to be hereafter. The seven stars in my right hand and the seven golden lampstands represent the seven churches.'

"Then the Christ gave me a message for each of the churches, including yours here in Ephesus. I have written down the messages to the churches. I will need your help and that of the church to have copies made for circulation among them. Each church should profit by hearing the messages to the others, as well as the one designated for itself. Perhaps churches in other areas will also want copies.

"Alexander, I saw more on Patmos. I was given a glimpse at the last page of human history. I have been privileged to see what will be hereafter and its spells victory, victory, victory!—victory for good, victory for God, and victory for the gospel! I've determined, dear brother, to write a Christian apocalypse—a veiled message. It will be in a sort of code. It will contain both literal and symbolic elements. In this way it will be unintelligible to the Roman authorities should it fall into their hands. Yet it will be intelligible and meaningful to believers who are familiar with Jewish apocalyptic literature such as the book of Daniel's prophecy. My purpose in writing this revelation is to encourage persecuted believers. The risen Lord commanded me to write the message, for their benefit. Great and terrible things are about to come upon the church, Alexander. I want to say to them, 'Sursum Corda'—lift up your hearts!

"It has been six years now since I completed my Gospel account and my three short circular letters to the churches. The messages to the seven churches of Asia and the apocalypse will complete my ministry of writing. Alexander, my young brother, should I climb the martyr's steep ascent to glory before the apocalypse is complete, will you finish it for me, on the basis of what I relate to you? Thank you! Thank you! I am anxious that this important message not be left incomplete. I do feel that it can encourage the churches, till the Lord comes.

"You know I was the youngest of the twelve, and as far as I know I may be the last alive. My brother James was the first of us to go. He met his death at the command of Herod whom our Lord once called, 'that old fox.' Andrew was slain in Greece across the Agean. Thomas went far to the east as messenger of the good news, and we haven't heard from him in years. There were earlier reports of his success in planting the gospel there. When I returned from Patmos, I was saddened to learn that both Simon Peter and Missionary Paul have died in Rome—Peter by crucifixion and Paul by decapitation. I fear, Alexander, that the fate befalling the church's leaders will soon come upon the church as a whole. Demonic powers will not take the church's success lying down. While I'm no pessimist, it's all too clear that days of testing are at hand. As for me, in the words of Paul's last letter, 'the time of my departure is at hand and I am ready to be offered,' poured in sacrifice, if it so pleases the Lord God.

"My, but the smell of that fish being smoked reminds me of days in Galilee! They seem so long ago and far away. You know, of course, that my brother James, my father Zebedee, and I were fishermen on the Sea of Galilee (which the Romans call Lake Tiberias). Our mother, Salome, was a sister of Mary of Nazareth, Jesus' mother. These crow's feet came around my eyes from squinting into the bright sun reflecting off the water there. The truth is I was never a very good fisherman. As long as the lake's waters were calm I was all right. But when there was the least storm (and there were often violent ones), I was the first man to get seasick. I'd loose my toes! I remember how impatient my brother would get with me, for my work was added to his in hauling in the nets and rowing.

"I shall never forget the call of Jesus to be his disciple. It wasn't just an impulsive decision. We had heard our cousin from Nazareth preach a number of times in Galilee—at Nazareth (wow, that was a service to remember!) and at Capernaum. Even before the beginning of his ministry, James and I had become disciples of John the Baptist. It was the imprisonment of John, of course, that signaled the beginning of Jesus' ministry. He called us that day from mending our nets. His words were graphic, 'You are fishers. I will make you fishers of men.' He later told us that he called us to be with him, and that he might send us forth to preach the good news of the kingdom. After his death, resurrection, and ascension his ministry was committed to us and through the twelve to speak to men like you. So the message will continue to spread from spark, until he returns.

"I'd like to tell you many things about those days with the Master. But time will not allow, and I've set much of it down along with my studied reflection, in my Gospel account.

"Do let me tell you about Jesus' nickname for James and me. He called us, 'sons of thunder.' It was not a highly complimentary handle but an accurate one I'm afraid. You see we were a highly ambitious pair, and on top of that our mother Salome was ambitious for us. I suppose every mother wants to see her boys do well and make a place for themselves in life. We shared our excitement about Jesus and the kingdom with her. One day she went with us to talk with the Master. We tried to get a commitment from him to grant our request before we stated it. The request was that we be named his first and second ministers or cabinet members, once he established the kingdom.

"Our request was not so unreasonable as it might sound on the surface. For one thing the disciple band was a rather rag-tag group. Most of the twelve were men of very common means. James and I were from a fairly well-to-do family. Our father Zebedee owned a fishing fleet and he had hired servants who carried on the business after James and I went into full-time religious work. Further, our father had contributed financially to the support of Jesus' work. All this was due some consideration we felt. Still further, there was the matter of our kinship with the Master—which is no small matter in the East. After all, blood is thicker than water, you know. We felt that our joint request for preference was quite in order.

"I remember Jesus' gentle rebuke. He said, 'You don't know what you ask.' And as it turned out we really didn't understand that his kingdom was to be a spiritual and not a military one. Jesus went on to say, 'He who would be greatest in the kingdom must be servant of all.' That was a reversal of the world's standards and frankly, it was puzzling to us for a long time. Only in later years did we come to see what he meant. I'm sure Jesus' standard is one that many Christians will find hard to meet—yet it is essential for true discipleship.

"Another reason the Master called us 'sons of thunder' was that we had quick tempers. I recall an occasion when we were enroute from Galilee to Jerusalem. There seemed an urgency in Jesus' manner and we took the shortest way, going through Samaria. He sent the two of us on ahead of the party to arrange lodging for the night. Since James and I were the youngest of the twelve, we often drew such assignments. The Samaritans were plainly rude and refused us lodging. It was a simple case of racial and religious prejudice on their part. Prejudice is an ugly thing, Alexander, especially when you are its victim! We were outraged! We hurried back to Jesus and the band. 'Master,' we asked, 'shall we call down fire from heaven and destroy these inhospitable people?'

" 'No,' said Jesus. And we went on to another village.

"It was ironic, Alexander, that after Pentecost, deacon Philip was led by the Spirit to preach in Samaria. His words met with a ready and sympathetic response. Large crowds heard him, miracles were performed, and many came to believe in Jesus as Lord.

The apostles and church in Jerusalem heard that Samaria had accepted the word of God. They sent Peter and me down to Samaria to verify these reports. We found that indeed they had become believers and had been baptized by Philip in the name of the Lord Jesus. We laid hands on the new converts and they received the Holy Spirit. It was much like the experience of the believers here in Ephesus when Paul came on his first visit. You will recall how the dozen believers had been baptized with John's baptism and hadn't heard of the Holy Spirit! There was an episode with Simon the magician in Samaria, but that's another story. The point is that where I had once wanted to call down lightning to destroy people, I later prayed down the fire of the Holy Spirit on them! How different is the pleasure of God.

"There were other occasions that earned our nickname, 'sons of thunder.' Once we came upon a fellow who was healing the sick in Jesus' name. When we checked him out, we learned that he did not even belong to our disciple group—so we forbade him to heal in Jesus' name. After all, he wasn't one of us. That night at dinner I bragged to Jesus about what we'd done. Much to my surprise Jesus said, 'Forbid him not. He that is not against us is for us.' I learned that the Jesus movement is bigger than I'd thought.

"It is true that James and I, along with Peter, were members of the inner circle within the disciple band. Only the three of us were present with Jesus at the raising of Jairus' daughter. We three were also the only ones present at the transfiguration of Jesus. We saw him glorified and heard him talk with Moses and Elijah on the mountaintop. I recall how Peter wanted to stay up there. Well, the truth is we all did. It was so marvelous, much like my visions on Patmos.

"We three were also present with Jesus at his time of agony in Gethsemane, though we weren't much comfort to him. We were all bone-weary from the week's controversy and hostility. However, as you know, worse agony, much worse, was to come.

"Alexander, I do hope I have opportunity to tell you about the events of that last week. I was at the table with the Master in the upper room of John Mark's mother's house, at Passover. I'll never forget how I felt when he said, 'One of you shall betray me.' That was an awesome time of heart searching, I'll tell you!

"I was present at Jesus' crucifixion and heard him say, 'Behold, your mother.' As you know, I cared for Mary until her death, here in Ephesus.

"I was the first of the twelve to arrive at the empty tomb on that first Easter morning. I outran old stubby-legged Peter. But brash fellow that he always was, he was the first to enter the tomb and verify that Jesus' body was indeed not there.

"Well, Alexander, as you can see, I'm an old man and I'm prone to ramble on endlessly.

"Do let me say this, my young brother. Believers in the Christ need not fear death. I've had a glimpse of glory. It is absolutely indescribable! I intend to try to describe my vision of heaven in the apocalypse—with the most extravagant language at my command. But my poor words will prove as inadequate as trying to explain to an unborn child the beauty of a sunset or the fragrance of a rose!

"Alexander, my message to the young church is, 'Love one another.' That's the heart of our faith.

"What? What's tnat? How did a son of thunder become the beloved disciple? Oh, that's an easy one to answer. You see Jesus called us to be with him. You can't be with him very long and remain the same. Living in his presence is life-transforming.

"Remember, Alexander, tell your people: 'Love one another! Love one another!' "

PART III
Expressing Discipleship

10
Expressing Discipleship Through Church Life

Ephesians 4; 2 Corinthians 8 to 9

God has called us all to be disciples, disciplined ones. Discipline for some of us has a negative ring. We remember that discipline in school usually meant punishment. If you were disciplined, you were sent to the office of the superintendent or the principal, and the rule of learning was applied in a way to leave a stinging reminder that you'd better shape up.

In the Bible discipline does not carry a negative note. It's positive. A disciple is one who learns, who harnesses resources in order to do what God has called him to do. Discipleship is expressed in many different ways to enrich life, through our personal witness, through family life, through our church, through daily work and play, and through citizenship. One of the richest biblical themes concerns expressing discipleship through a church.

The Bible is so filled with information about what a church ought to be and do that it's difficult to single out and concentrate on any one passage. But two key portions are found in Ephesians 4 and 2 Corinthians 8 and 9. These are church-centered epistles. Ephesians describes the church as the body of Christ. Corinthians deals with certain specific problems in the church at Corinth.

In Ephesians Paul wrote, "It was he who 'gave gifts to men'; he appointed some to be apostles, others to be prophets, others to be evangelists, others to be pastors and teachers. He did this to prepare all God's people for the work of Christian service, to build up the body of Christ. And so we shall all come together to that oneness in our faith and in our knowledge of the Son of God; we shall become mature men, reaching to the very height of Christ's full stature. Then we shall no longer be children, carried by the waves and blown about by every shifting wind of the teaching of deceitful men, who lead others to error by the tricks they invent. Instead, by speaking the truth in a spirit of love, we must grow up in every way to Christ, who is the head. Under his control all the different parts of the body fit together, and the whole body is held together by every joint with which it is provided. So when each separate part works as it should, the whole body grows and builds itself up through love" (4:11-16, TEV).

In 2 Corinthians 8 and 9 these passages speak about church and discipleship: "I am not laying down any rules. But by showing how eager others are to help, I am trying to find out how real your own love is. For you know the grace of our Lord Jesus Christ; rich as he was, he made himself poor for your sake, in order to make you rich by means of his poverty.

"This is my opinion on the matter: it is better for you to finish now what you began last year. You were the first, not only to act, but also to be willing to act. On with it, then, and finish the job! Be as eager to finish it as you were to plan it, and do it with what you have. If you are eager to give, God will accept your gift on the basis of what you have to give, not on what you don't have. I am not trying to relieve others by putting a burden on you; but since you have plenty at this time, it is only fair that you should help those who are in need. Then, when you are in need and they have plenty, they will help you. In this way both are treated equally" (8:8-14, TEV).

"Remember this: the man who plants few seeds will have a small crop; the one who plants many seeds will have a large crop. Each one should give, then, as he has decided, not with regret or out of a sense of duty; for God loves the one who gives gladly. And God is able to give you more than you need, so that you will always have all you need for yourselves and more than enough for every good cause. As the scripture says, 'He gives generously to the poor; his kindness lasts forever.' And God, who supplies seed for the sower and bread to eat, will also supply you with all the seed you need and make it grow, to produce a rich harvest from your generosity" (9:6-10, TEV).

Church life calls for discipline. In the old days whenever you discussed church discipline, it meant kicking somebody out of the church because of something he had done the church generally didn't agree with. If someone were caught dancing on Saturday night, they might be "churched," disciplined, removed from the rolls. If someone were caught drinking, gambling, or committing adultery, they were usually disciplined. Fellowship was withdrawn from them.

The Roman Catholic Church practices a form of church discipline in excommunication. The church takes away the sacraments from a person. Since many Catholics believe that the sacraments are essential to spiritual growth and life eternal, it is a devastating thing to be disciplined in the Roman Catholic Church. In the New Testament some direction is given to Christians to pull away from those living lives unbecoming to a follower of Christ, but mainly the concept of the disciple is one of self-discipline.

I.

The Bible says that *one aspect of expressing discipleship through church life is for believers to assemble together*. It's not biblically accurate to say, "Let's go to church," because church isn't a place, it's people. When you say to someone, "Come go to church with me," or, "I've got to go to church tonight," you leave the wrong impression. You imply that a building is the church, or a program is the church, or some kind of activity is the church. In the Bible the church was always the people, the people of God, the ones God called.

If someone asks you during the week, "Where is your church?" to be biblically accurate you should point to the entire community and say, "There's where my church is." If you don't want to be considered some kind of a nut, however, you should probably direct them to the building where you meet on Sunday and say, "There's where it is."

Biblically, church means people, not place. Yet in the New Testament, the people were commanded to come together, to assemble. Coming together requires discipline. It's not always easy on Sunday morning to get up, dress, and travel to associate with the people of God. It's much easier to sleep late, read the funny papers, eat a leisurely breakfast, and watch a football game on television. On Sunday night it's easier to stay in, get ready for the week, and relax than get out and go to meetings. Many people just don't quite make the gathering of the family of faith, at least not consistently. The reason is not that they are evil, deep in depravity. It is primarily that they are not disciplined.

Gathering the body of Christ together is primarily a discipline matter. It's saying, "I *will* get up. I *will* go. I *will* do what's necessary to get me from place A to place B where other people are coming together." Some of us are quite proud of ourselves whenever we make a special effort. It's raining, cold, windy, and we've had company late the night before—but we go to the meeting house anyway.

One Sunday morning I had to drive several miles to preach

in a city other than where I lived. It was a cold, icy, winter morning. I scraped ice off my windshield, huddled in the cold car, and headed out. The roads were slick and I narrowly averted a serious wreck. I thought, "How proud God must be of me to get out in weather like this and risk my life to go meet with the people of God." Then I remembered what price he had paid to make possible my salvation: his Son died on a cross for me. I realized there was no cause for my sense of sacrifice. I was doing only what's expected of me. I deserved no special honor or merit. I was being a disciple, one who disciplines himself enough to do whatever is necessary to follow God's will. The Bible says that we're not to forsake the assembling of ourselves together, and that where two or three are gathered together Christ is in the midst of us. It's important that we get together.

Quite a few people wonder about us, particularly those of us who come together on Sunday night for Bible study, worship, and Christian fellowship. They question if we are quite bright, if there isn't something peculiar about people who gather in a church building when they could stay home, or be out partying with friends, or go to bed early. Well, it's not really a matter of comfort, pleasure, or convenience. It's a matter of discipline.

Getting together with Christian friends at a church house is not to be compared with deeds of heroic sacrifice, of course. It is not a distasteful, dangerous, or disagreeable experience. Actually those who assemble on a regular basis find it quite delightful. Fun, fellowship, Christian growth, and spiritual feasting are there for those who gather. But overcoming inertia and going is quite often a matter of discipline. Few Christians have never thought, "I just don't want to go." A difference between the "disciple" and the "church member" is that the disciple will come regularly even when he doesn't feel like it or want to.

Such discipline is important for us because in gathering together we grow in Christ, learn from one another, read from the Word, grow a fellowship, share common experiences of worship, provide for a wide variety of needs and ages in a way small groups cannot, and make possible a program of world missions. In no other meeting can you gain and give what you can gain and give by being in an assembly of believers—not in recreation in God's fresh air, or in solitude enjoying the beauty of a sunrise or a sunset, or by good Christian fellowship apart from the whole of the body of Christ. The New Testament stresses the importance of the body of Christ, of each member being present to carry out an assigned task. Surely it is not difficult to see why. The body can't function properly with missing parts; neither can the body of Christ.

II.

The second way *discipleship is expressed through church life is in developing the gifts God grants us for ministry*. All God's children are gifted. In the Ephesians correspondence, Paul puts it quite bluntly: God has gifted everyone who is a member of the body of Christ. People have different gifts, but all are for the purpose of ministry. No gift is ever developed or properly used apart from discipline. The Bible is a gift from God. You don't learn to study the Bible, understand it, and have the rich meaning of it fill your life apart from disciplined study. It takes time, effort, prayer. You can't expect simply to open the Bible nonchalantly from time to time and get from it what God has for you.

What is true of the Bible is true of other kinds of God-given gifts, such as ministry, teaching, bearing witness, and sharing with others. It takes the discipline of continuous use, practice, and development if gifts are to be properly used. Some people after years of teaching Sunday School, or serving in leadership positions, or singing in the choir feel like they deserve to be relieved. "I'll let somebody else do that awhile and I'll take a back seat," they say. Or when they move to another town they think, "I'll just lay out awhile and not get as involved in church work here as I have been." The Bible indicates nobody takes a back seat in God's business. We're all supposed to be involved as ministers, using the gifts God granted us. Like an unused muscle, a gift not used begins to dissipate.

Everybody ought to be in a place of ministry and service. The discipline of attending is important but it must be linked with the discipline of developing our gifts in service. Are you a better teacher this year than you were last year? A better witness? A better Bible student? A better sharer of the good news? A better choir member? A better pianist? A better organist? Year by year through discipline we grow better and better in our ability to serve.

III.

The third way of *expressing discipleship through church life is in regard to doctrine.* Paul told the Ephesian Christians that they must grow up and not be tossed about by every wind of doctrine. In other correspondence, he warned again and again that there would be people who would come with strange doctrines to lure believers away from the central faith. Maintaining doctrinal stability has always been a problem in the Christian movement. It's very difficult for any church consistently to emphasize a balanced whole in regard to biblical truth. In the limited time for worship and Bible study only a few themes can be touched.

Inevitably when there is a vacuum caused by a truth left unemphasized somebody will come along and say, "You see, that church is not really a Bible-believing church. They don't stress this doctrine!" Then they begin to build an entire movement, a complete theology, on that one omission. Many denominations and churches have been started by people who saw a doctrinal vacuum and rushed in to fill it. By overemphasizing a particular doctrine, they develop a kind of heresy.

I trust that in our fellowship we will always have the totality of the gospel, that we will never omit any essential part of it. But everyone should realize we can't stress everything all the time. Simply because the Holy Spirit is not mentioned in every service and sermon fifteen times does not mean we don't believe in the Holy Spirit. Because we don't allude to the authority of the Bible at least fifteen times in every meeting doesn't mean we don't believe in the Bible. Because we don't say "evangelism" thirty-six times in each lesson doesn't mean we don't believe in evangelism. Yet, if you never hear reference to these, something is wrong.

The totality of the Bible needs to be proclaimed. The people of God who keep doctrine sound help a church move ahead. The splits in the New Testament fellowships were caused by people who took some aspect of doctrine and blew it out of proportion or who began to prey on the fancies, fears, and superstitions of Christians, feeding them a doctrinal diet that really wasn't from God at all. A lot of that goes on today.

Disciplined effort is required to determine what is of God and what is not, what is from the Word and what is not, what is sound doctrine and what is sorry doctrine. Such discernment demands maturity which comes by prayer, worship, Bible study, and careful study. Otherwise you are liable to be washed away by some wave of strange teaching which comes across your life.

Most of us have itchy ears. We like to hear something that's new. "Never heard that before! I like that!" we exclaim. Well, just because you've never heard it before doesn't make it true. In fact, the fact you haven't heard it before ought to raise a question. If you have gone to church meetings for thirty or forty years, you've just about heard most of what's true. If you haven't, you've been going to the wrong church. So don't always be seeking something new and different. Anybody who tries to come up with the far out, the outlandish, the concept nobody ever thought of before is missing the point. Paul kept preaching again and again the same simple gospel—Christ died for our sins; God was in Christ reconciling the world unto himself; repent, believe, be saved, and mature in your knowledge of God.

Most everything that is going to be discovered about the essential doctrines of the Bible has already been stated. There's really not a whole lot new that will come out. Of course, we should constantly strive to gain new insights, to discover how the Bible relates to us and our world. Truth needs to be restated in light of changing settings. Scholarship is important. The danger rests in the push to be different, to proclaim an insight no one has ever had before. "Come, join us and our movement; we've found the real meaning of the Bible, truth nobody else has ever had," someone declares. And people will flock to him, simply because what is proposed sounds new, different, fresh.

My first few years at seminary were spent discovering "new" truths about the Bible, convinced no one else had ever found them. Every time I thought I had something new, however, I would go to a church history or theology class and find it had been stated clearly by Christians in former times or declared heresy centuries ago. I'm grateful that I live resting on the bedrock of doctrine established by great Christians of the past who've handed down to us what may seem old-fashioned, stuffy, and routine but is true nonetheless.

Discipline of doctrine is important, but I don't think that means we ought to be heresy hunters, snooping around to find somebody guilty of erroneous doctrine. It does mean that we are responsible for the growth of our own Christian life and understanding of true doctrine. Unfortunately some have been Christians for quite some time but still don't know a good doctrine from a bad one when they see it. They don't enjoy enough grounding in the Scriptures, church history, and the wonderful heritage which is ours as Baptists to know when they stumble across an untruth or a heresy. Discipline will help correct such a shortcoming.

IV.

Finally, discipleship *is expressed through church life by giving*. We can discipline ourselves to assemble together regularly. We can discipline ourselves to develop our gifts. We can discipline our minds to distinguish true doctrine from bad doctrine. But unless we also discipline ourselves in giving so that the gospel can be proclaimed throughout the world, the other aspects of discipleship will be to no avail.

Paul wrote to the Christians at Corinth stressing the importance of giving, asking them to put aside their gifts on the first day of the week as God had prospered. I realize that everyone cannot lay aside on the first day of the week in the same way because earnings come in at different times and in various ways. Nevertheless, there is a consistent pattern of giving based on discipline which develops strong stewardship and contributes to effective church ministry.

Haphazardness is one of our worst problems in regard to stewardship. A person is absent a Sunday and forgets to turn in an offering envelope. "Oh, well," he says, "I'll make it up next week." Next week comes, and he forgets again. He falls farther and farther behind. When he gets a statement from the church near the end of the year as to where he stands in regard to his pledge, he protests, "I just can't make it up now. I'm too far behind. God surely will understand, and if I can carry forward losses on income tax surely I can carry forward behindness on tithing." It doesn't work that way. It is the consistent, disciplined giving of the people of God that makes possible the consistent, disciplined proclamation of the word of God.

God has promised to meet our needs if we are generous with what we have. I like the way Paul put it when he wrote to the Corinthians. "Remember this: the man who plants few seeds will have a small crop; the one who plants many seeds will have a large crop. Each one should give, then, as he has decided, not with regret or out of a sense of duty; for God loves the one who gives gladly. And God is able to give you more than you need, so that you will always have all you need for yourselves and more than enough for every good cause" (2 Cor. 9:6-8, TEV). The Bible clearly teaches that you can't outgive God.

No church has ever grown great without discipline. It's clear that many churches have members who are truly disciples. Large crowds in worship services, faithful attendance at committee meetings, careful preparation for teaching Sunday School lessons, ministering to human hurt, and leading training groups, consistent visitation and witness, widespread development of gifts, and sacrificial stewardship are evidences of the kind of discipline through churchmanship that the world needs more of. Perhaps you're one of life's undisciplined ones in church and other realms—the kind of person who can't pass the dessert tray without taking some, who always promises to start an exercise program tomorrow but never does, who insists you are going to keep good financial records next year but don't. Start right now being a disciple, a disciplined one, in regard to church—coming together with fellow believers, developing gifts as a minister, studying to be able to determine correct doctrine, and sharing your material resources with others.

11
Expressing Discipleship Through Witness

Matthew 28:18-20; Acts 1:6-11

We Baptists have talked a great deal about evangelism and missions. We've exhorted one another concerning stewardship, tithing, and fiscal responsibility. Now we are beginning more extensive discussions in the area of discipleship. Emphasis on discipleship is biblical. Those who first followed Jesus were known not as "believers" nor as "Christians" nor as "church members." They were known as "disciples," disciplined ones.

A disciple is a person who follows someone in whom he believes and trusts. A disciple believes in the person he follows so much that he wants everybody else to know about him, follow him, trust him. Further, the disciple is willing to work—to pay whatever price necessary—to carry out his leader's wishes, teachings, and commands.

We've said much about reading the Bible. Quite frankly the Bible is not to be read merely for our own personal edification but to equip us to be disciples. We talk a great deal about prayer. Yet prayer is not so much a way to get what we want from God as it is a means to discover what God wants from us as disciples of Jesus. The exercises of piety are not ends in themselves but means to the end of our becoming better disciples.

Discipleship is expressed in a number of ways. It's expressed in our witness. It's expressed in our church life. It's expressed in our families. It's expressed in the way we conduct our public life in the spheres of recreation, work, and citizenship. But basically discipleship begins with how we relate the good news about Christ to other people.

A disciple is one who shares the good news. Being a witness is not an option for the child of God. It's required. It's not an elective course. It's mandatory. It's not something you can choose to do or not do according to your fancy. If you have given yourself to him, you'll want to share him and that's what witnessing is about. Jesus had much to say to his disciples about expressing discipleship through witnessing.

According to the Gospel of Matthew, in his last personal confrontation with his disciples, Jesus said, "Go ye therefore, and teach all nations, baptizing them in the name of the Father, and of the Son, and of the Holy Ghost: teaching them to observe all things whatsoever I have commanded you: and lo, I am with you alway, even unto the end of the world" (Matt. 28:19-20, KJV). The book of Acts opens with Jesus outside the city of Jerusalem giving his disciples a parting command, an injunction of departure: "When they therefore were come together, they asked of him, saying, Lord, wilt thou at this time restore again the kingdom to Israel? And he said unto them, It is not for you to know the times or the seasons, which the Father hath put in his own power. But ye shall receive power, after that the Holy Ghost is come upon you: and you shall be witnesses unto me both in Jerusalem, and in all Judea, and in Samaria, and unto the uttermost part of the earth. And when he had spoken these things, while they beheld, he was taken up; and a cloud received him out of their sight. And while they looked stedfastly toward heaven as he went up, behold, two men stood by them in white apparel; which also said, Ye men of Galilee, why stand ye gazing up into heaven? this same Jesus, which is taken up from you into heaven, shall so come in like manner as ye have seen him go into heaven" (Acts 1:6-11, KJV).

I.

There are four aspects about expressing our discipleship through witness that these passages stress. One is *the source of power for our witness.* Many people fear to share the good news because they feel powerless and weak. Have you ever hesitated to speak to someone about his relationship to God in Christ because you were afraid of what he would say to you? Or what he would think about you? Or perhaps you held back from sharing because you feared what might be asked you—questions you'd never pondered, or worse, those you'd pondered and found no satisfactory answer for. You were afraid that you'd let your Lord down or embarrass yourself. Therefore, you followed the course of least resistance and did not say anything at all about Jesus Christ.

For those paralyzed by powerlessness and fear the Bible gives hope. You don't witness on your own. You do it with the power of the Holy Spirit. Jesus said, "But ye shall receive power, after that the Holy Ghost is come upon you."

The New Testament clearly teaches that the Holy Spirit comes into our life when we trust Jesus as Savior and that he fills our life more and more as we become more and more committed to Jesus as Lord. The Holy Spirit is a gift of salvation, but the Holy Spirit's domain in our life expands as we grow in Christ. The Holy Spirit comes to everyone who repents of sin and has faith in Christ. If you have trusted Christ for salvation, you don't need to pray that God will give you the Holy Spirit. He already has.

Some of us, however, have very little capacity for the Holy

Spirit in our life. We have not prayed enough, we have not shared Christ with others enough, we have not studied the Word of God enough for the spiritual walls of our life to be pushed back enough for the Holy Spirit to have a large place. To the degree the Holy Spirit fills us, we have power to do what God has commissioned us to do in Jesus Christ, to share the good news. So part of our responsibility. as witnesses is to become disciples, learners, disciplined ones. The book of Acts reveals that when the Holy Spirit becomes so much a part of us that he guides and directs us, witnessing becomes a natural part of our daily life. We will want to share because the Holy Spirit within us wants to share. We will have the courage to confront people with the claims of the gospel because the Spirit gives us courage that we don't have on our own. The Holy Spirit will give us insights into how to reach out to other persons and to share the gospel with them. The Holy Spirit will direct us to the people with whom we are to share Christ.

Many people misemphasize the ministry of the Holy Spirit. Some stress that the Holy Spirit is to make your tongue speak in strange sounds. But as Paul said, "I had rather speak five words with my understanding, that by my voice I might teach others also, than ten thousand words in an unknown tongue" (1 Cor. 14:19, KJV). Some emphasize that the Holy Spirit is to give an ecstatic feeling, an emotional upsurge that causes you to clap your hands or stomp your feet or sway your body. You can do all those things without the aid of the Holy Spirit. The Holy Spirit's concern is not that you clap your hands but that you minister to others with those hands, not that you shuffle your feet in some ecstatic display but that your feet take you to persons who need to know Jesus, not that you sway your body but that you "present your bodies a living sacrifice, holy, acceptable unto God" (Rom. 12:1, KJV).

Quite frankly, many mature Christians have a funny feeling in the pit of the stomach when they go to tell others about Jesus. Our culture is basically antireligious. We are told again and again that religion is a personal, private matter, and we shouldn't dabble in other people's personal, private affairs. People who openly share their faith are met with raised eyebrows and muttered character descriptions such as "fanatic," "religious nut," or "over-zealous." In such a setting, we need all the help we can get to break us out of our shell and move us to confront other people with the good news. Take heart. You don't have to do it alone. The Holy Spirit will help you. The purpose of the Holy Spirit, according to the Bible, is to break down the walls which separate us from persons and to empower, enable, guide, and encourage us to share the good news of Jesus Christ. Our outreach and evangelism efforts, our missions and ministry thrusts in the name of Jesus will be like a rocket that misfires on the launch pad if we don't learn to let our lives be filled with the Spirit of God who gives power.

II.

The second aspect of expressing discipleship through witness these verses emphasize is that *the extent of our concern is immense.* In the Matthew account there is a rhythmic repetition of infinities—*all* power, *all* nations, *all* things, *alway*, even unto the *end of the world.* In the book of Acts the geographic extent is stressed—witnesses in Jerusalem, Judea, Samaria, and unto the uttermost part of the earth. In both Matthew and Acts the concept is the same—the extent of our concern is the whole world and everybody in it.

Missions is at the heart of witness. We can never be content with sharing the good news only with people in our community. We must get the word out to people far away from us. That's why it's important that we give money, sons and daughters, ourselves, time, energies, and talents for mission activities, trips, and experiences.

In concentrating on "to the uttermost," let's not forget "in Jerusalem." We are to share the good news in our own backyard with people with whom we work, go to school, and confront in social activity. If we put all of our emphasis on going to people we have never seen before, we will miss the great opportunity God puts before us every day to share the good news with those we know. As I talk with people who respond during the invitation time I've been deeply impressed with how many come to know Christ because somebody they knew told them about him. "Jerusalem," their here and now, was the point of their recovery of hope. With whom have you shared Christ this week? What member of your family? What neighbor? What work associate? What person in school? Have you become what Jesus said we would become when the Holy Spirit comes into our life—witnesses?

The extent of witness concern is infinite—everybody, everywhere, at all times. But the everybody, everywhere, and at all times begins with somebody here and now. I've noticed that many of us have a great failing. We're so busy dreaming grand schemes, plotting immense maneuvers, and discovering how we can win the entire world that we run right past the person we work with who is lost, we live beside who is not a Christian, we go to school with who has never known Jesus. All of our talk, dreams, and visions of extensive witness efforts are to God an abysmal mess if we don't have concern for the people we make contact with every day. The extent of our concern is the neighbor next door, the person in the office, the individual in study hall, as well as the people who live on the continents of the earth and the islands of the sea, who dwell in urban ghettos and Indian reservations, who populate the prisons and jails.

III.

A third aspect of expressing discipleship through witness is the *action-centered nature of the task.* The Bible to me is an exciting book because it speaks with such forcefulness about action. When you read in the Bible about the nature of our task as disciples, you discover that it's an action-oriented adventure. Witnessing is not so much something you study, ponder, or pray about as it's something you do. Listen to the verbs used in these passages: "go," "teach," "baptize," "be."

The Christian who expresses discipleship through witnessing must "go." You can't be a witness if you stay in one place. Even an invalid can witness by "going" outside himself. Witnessing begins with going. Go outside the walls of the church! Go outside your own Christian family circle! Go! We have had a tendency to emphasize the "come." Come to church with me. Come to my Sunday School fellowship. Come hear our choir. The "come" of witness is important, but it's the "go" of the gospel that makes the difference.

A people-centered church must never forget the going as well as the coming. Go and tell. Go and share. Go to where the people are. People who are lost don't come to church buildings much anymore on their own. People seldom drop in on Sunday School classes and say, "Oh, I'm so excited to be here for the first time." Some church members enjoy the fellowship with other Christians so much that they don't want to go visit the lost or see new people come into the church. Such an attitude is contrary to the "go" which Jesus commanded.

"Teach" is another verb which describes the nature of the witness responsibility. "Teach them to observe all things whatsoever I have commanded you," Jesus said. We have a responsibility not only to share how a person is to be saved but also how a saved person is to live. Evangelism and Christian nurture must go hand in hand. That's why we are committed to Christian education, programs of development, and Bible study.

The third verb which describes the nature of our witness task is "baptize." Used in Matthew primarily to mean making converts, baptism is seen as an expression of faith in Christ. In most churches today people are asked to come down the aisle and publicly profess belief in Jesus and then later be baptized. In the New Testament, there's little if any indication people came down aisles in services to profess Christ publicly. Instead, baptism was the primary means of publicly declaring faith in Jesus Christ. Baptisms were usually performed in public and were a means of openly professing allegiance to Christ.

Baptism was not thought of as necessary for salvation by the first believers. It was not considered a sacrament. It was not seen as essential for cleansing of sin. It was not viewed as an absolutely necessary ingredient for admission into the kingdom of God. But it was the way that people said to the world, "I have died to an old way of life and I have come alive to the life in Christ. I have identified with the One who, when put into the grave, rose from the dead." Baptism was a declaration of faith. It marked the end of an old way of life and the beginning of a new way. In a time when Christians were often persecuted, baptism was not taken lightly, it required conviction and courage. I'm glad to be a Baptist, to be part of a people who take baptism seriously and use a mode that shows death to an old way and birth to a new one, that identifies with Christ who died for us and who rose from the dead for our sins. No other way can picture that except immersion.

Another verb used in describing the disciples' witness is "be." "Ye shall *be* witnesses," Jesus said. It's not so much a matter of

what we say as who we are. We are to be the people of God.
We are to be living audiovisual aids of what Jesus Christ has
done and can do for a person. Christ in you is the hope of glory.
Be a witness. Be a sharer of Jesus Christ.

IV.

The final point made in these passages about expressing discipleship through witness is *the fruit of our labor.* In Matthew
the promise of the fruit of the labor is, "I am with you alway,
even unto the end." The person who is expressing discipleship
through witness knows the daily presence of the living Lord. Jesus
promised his followers, "I'll send the Holy Spirit. He'll be your
guide and comforter. The Holy Spirit will be my representative
in your life. The Spirit will give you power. To the degree you
live in the Spirit, you will be aware of my presence."

When someone tells you, "God seems so far off, so distant,
so unreal that I find it difficult to believe in him," you are likely
listening to a person who hasn't been sharing Christ with others.
Like a muscle which grows flabby with disuse, the Spirit of God
shrinks inside of us when not called on. When you realize that
the Holy Spirit was given to us for the primary purpose of making
us effective witnesses, you begin to understand why so many
people have a shriveled spirit in their lives. If you want to know
the joy of the presence of the Holy Spirit, if you want to know
the comfort that Christ is with you always, then practice the
daily sharing of Christ with other people.

Acts records the promise of the fruit of the Christian's labor
also. The account begins with the statement, "And while they
looked stedfastly toward heaven as he went up, behold, two men
stood by them in white apparel." I would have been gazing up
into heaven, too. What a startling sight! The disciples had already
been dazzled by Jesus' habit of doing the unpredictable. He came

alive after being crucified and buried. He walked through doors. He prepared food for them, and they watched him eat with hands still pierced from the nails on the cross. Then, without warning, as they walked along he suddenly began to rise into the sky. Gawking toward the heavens, they were startled by the words which came from two who stood by them: "Why stand ye gazing up into heaven? this same Jesus which is taken up from you into heaven, shall so come in like manner as ye have seen him go into heaven." The promise of the fruit of our labor is that as we share the risen and ascended Christ with others he'll come back again to claim us someday.

The emphasis in the New Testament concerning the coming again of Christ is not on when he is coming but on what we are to do in preparation. In fact, Jesus said, "It is not for you to know the times or the seasons, which the Father hath put in his own power" (Acts 1:7, KJV). If we attempt to use the Holy Spirit to figure out God's timetable or if we look upon the coming again of Christ as some sort of gimmick to determine future history, we've missed the point of it all. Peter showed us the proper response to the fact of Christ's coming again when he wrote, "What manner of persons ought ye to be in all holy conversation and godliness, looking for and hasting unto the coming of the day of God, wherein the heavens being on fire shall be dissolved, and the elements shall melt with fervent heat?" (2 Pet. 3:11-12, KJV). The response to that question is clear. We are to be witnesses, the faithful people of God sharing through word and action the good news about Jesus.

Does the coming again of Christ bother you? It should not. It is not intended to scare Christians but to give them encouragement and hope. "I'm coming back," was a promise, not a threat, for believers. In the meanwhile, don't try to figure out when. Don't be reading the signs of the times, instead expect him any time. Put your energy into witness, into sharing the good news so that people will be ready when he comes back. And what will be the fruit of your labor? To stand arm in arm with a great company of people who are safe in Christ because you witnessed and to hear him say, "Hey, you did a great job! Well done!"

Discipleship is expressed in numerous ways, but none is more important than through witnessing. You may be, as I am, tempted to show your discipleship in other ways—by church attendance, family life, community service, or personal ministry. Each of these is a phase of witness and important. But none takes the place of sharing the good news with others. If you are not already expressing your Christian discipleship through witness, begin today.

12
Expressing Discipleship Through Family Life

Deuteronomy 6:3-12

Before the people who followed Jesus were labeled Christians, they were called disciples. Before they were known as believers, they were referred to as disciples. Before the name *Baptist* was common, the term *disciple* was widely used. In fact, in the New Testament "disciple" is one of the first words used for the followers of Jesus.

Discipleship is important. It means learning about and following after Jesus Christ in all aspects of life. Discipleship should be expressed in every dimension of existence—in our personal attitudes, witness, church, family, community, work, leisure, and government.

No area of life should be shut off from discipleship. That's why Jesus talked to his followers about family and politics, why he discussed daily work and witness, why he walked with them through all of life's experiences. He shared with them—and us— that discipleship is to touch everything we are and everything that we'll ever be.

One important area of discipleship is family. A person cannot be a good Christian unless he is a good family member. No one can be all that God wants unless his family life is Christ saturated.

Husbands, wives, parents, children, in-laws, and relatives all have a responsibility to express Christian discipleship through family life.

In the sixth chapter of the book of Deuteronomy, God set forth for his people how they were to relate family life to his Word. The instructions are not out of date. True, this was for the people of Israel as they went into the Promised Land. It was to guide them as they inhabited that land. But these words also apply to us, the people of God, disciples of Jesus Christ, members of a church.

"Hear therefore, O Israel, and observe to do it; that it may be well with thee, and that ye may increase mightily, as the Lord God of thy fathers hath promised thee, in the land that floweth with milk and honey. Hear, O Israel: The Lord our God is one Lord: And thou shalt love the Lord thy God with all thine heart, and with all thy soul, and with all thy might. And these words, which I command thee this day, shall be in thine heart: and thou shalt teach them diligently unto thy children, and shalt talk of them when thou sittest in thine house, and when thou walkest by the way, and when thou liest down, and when thou risest up. And thou shalt bind them for a sign upon thine hand, and they shall be as frontlets between thine eyes. And thou shalt write them upon the posts of thy house, and on thy gates. And it shall be, when the Lord thy God shall have brought thee into the land which he sware unto thy fathers, to Abraham, to Isaac, and to Jacob, to give thee great and goodly cities, which thou buildest not, and houses full of all good things, which thou filledst not, and wells digged, which thou diggedst not, vineyards and olive trees, which thou plantedst not; when thou shalt have eaten and be full; then beware lest thou forget the Lord, which brought thee forth out of the land of Egypt, from the house of bondage" (Deut. 6:3-12, KJV).

In the New Testament there is also an emphasis on family life. The fifth and nineteenth chapters of Matthew, the seventh chapter of 1 Corinthians, the fifth and sixth chapters of Ephesians, and the third chapter of Colossians contain a special emphasis on family. In almost every part of the Bible God speaks to us from his Word about our families. No one who takes the Bible seriously can take family life lightly.

I.

According to the Bible, discipleship is to be expressed by the way we *help one another within families to grow spiritually, to learn about God's Word and about his ways.* That's what most of the sixth chapter of Deuteronomy is about—how the people of God were to learn about God within the family setting.

When the people of Israel were led from slavery into a nation by God, there was no temple. There were no synagogues. There were few places for religious meetings. Thus the main way in which the people could learn about God and his Word was through family life. One reason why Jewish families today are some of the most stable in all society may be because throughout history religious education among Jews centered in family life. Faith and family have been linked together. Religious devotion strengthened family life and families contributed to religious fervor.

If our devotion to God is to be strong, our families must be centers for developing religious commitment. If our families are to be stable, they must be rooted in religious experience. Many of our families are found wanting in regard to God's command that his Word be a constant companion in the household of faith. As recorded in Deuteronomy, when a person gets up in the morning he is to read the Scriptures or recite them from memory. As he goes about his work during the day he is to repeat verses of Scripture. The Word of God is to be a constant daily companion.

Because the Word of God was to be such a central feature in a Jewish family, Scriptures were to be visible at all times. Portions of Scripture were written on the doorposts or on little bits of parchment worn around wrists or the head. Later some Jews reduced those practices to mere ritual. They kept the letter of the command but forgot to fulfill its purpose. They wrote Scriptures on the doorposts and wore Scriptures around their wrists and heads, but they didn't put God's Word in their hearts. It's not enough to have the Bible visible—on a table, or shelf, or desk. We are also to read, ponder, and make it part of our life.

Day after day a family is to read the Bible, share the Bible, study the Bible, memorize the Bible, and quote the Bible, so that it becomes part of life—not an appendage to it. That's not easy to do. It is difficult to find a time in which the Scriptures can become a meaningful part of daily life. The Bible indicates it ought to be read when we rise up in the morning and when we go to bed at night, at the beginning and the end of each day. It ought to be part of those moments in which families are together before going out into the frantic activity of the work-a-day world and after coming home from involvement in that world.

But how many families make the Bible a consistent part of their daily life? How many families do begin and end the day with the Scriptures? How many families carry the Word of God in their minds and hearts so that they can share it with one another as crises come? If we could only become like God wants us to be, how much stronger would our lives, families, and churches be. With tragic consequences we let almost anything come in the way of that daily family time with the Word of God.

Parents are primarily responsible for the spiritual welfare of the family. The Bible says, "Thou shalt teach them diligently unto thy children." Children have a responsibility, however, to say to parents, "When will we study the Scriptures? When will we read

the Bible? When will we memorize the Word of God?" Parents
and youth working together like the pedals on a bicycle can keep
things moving along God's way within a family. Is it that way
in your house?

II.

The Bible also teaches that *we should express discipleship
through family by evangelism.* In the Old Testament the sharing
of the good news about God was not consistently done outside
the family of faith. The Jewish people had difficulty believing
that God really loved the whole world. When God called Jonah
to preach to Nineveh, for example, at first the prophet didn't
want to do it. But God continued to reveal that he was the God
of all, not just the God of Israel. The prophets of the eighth
century—Amos, Micah, Isaiah, and Hosea—clearly declared that
God, Yahweh, was not the tribal god of a small band of desert
wanderers. He was the God Creator, the God Sustainer, the God
Redeemer of all people.

God called Israel to the task of being the channel of redemption
to the world. When they resisted, God brought forth a shoot out
of the dying stump of Israel to become the source of the Messiah.
Jesus, the Savior of the world, was born from that branch of God's
people. The task of being evangels passed to us as Jesus' followers.
We are to share the good news with everybody, to be the channel
of redemption. In the early days of the Christian movement there
were no church buildings, no highly organized congregations, no
denominational agencies, no mission boards, no seminaries. The
first Christians evangelized and ministered within two basic structures, local churches and family units.

Paul wrote about "the church in thy house"—house churches.
The churches were a sort of extended family with a father, or
pastor, of the group. Other persons began to assume special re-

sponsibilities in that "family"—teachers, evangelists, proclaimers, ministers, and administrators—according to their gifts.

Primary family units also played a big part in the Christian mission in those first years. Early church leaders realized the family was the key to evangelism, Christian growth, and ministry. Evangelism in the future may also be done largely through families. Certainly the church will maintain a role of prominence. Revival meetings will continue to have a place. Visitation programs will reach certain people who will respond to the message of the gospel. But more and more evangelism will be done through family units—families living in apartment house complexes, families in neighborhoods, families in mobile home parks, families in recreation centers. It will be families through whom God works.

Few unsaved people come to church meetings unless they are visited, invited, and prayed for. With apartment houses increasing, both husband and wife working, leisure time opportunities expanding, and children's activities accelerating, typical church visitation programs are becoming less and less effective. A family ministry approach is called for in which each family in Christ serves as a center for witness and ministry among other families nearby. Cells of Christlike compassion, these families can make a difference in a mobile home park, apartment house, or suburban neighborhood.

And what kind of families will God be able to use? Families with a prayer list of people who are lost. Families who pray by name for people about whom they are concerned. Families who care about young people, children, adults, and the aging. Families who share the Word of God freely. Families who invite others to join them for Bible study. Families who share through example the joy of being in Christ Jesus.

Do you have that kind of family? Is your family an evangelistic unit—praying, reaching out, bringing in, visiting, expressing concern? Is the evidence of the gospel seen in your community, apartment house, or neighborhood because of your family?

III.

The Bible teaches that *discipleship is to be expressed through family life by worship.* In both the Old Testament and the New Testament worship was primarily a family affair. After the Temple was built, families worshiped in it on special religious occasions. When synagogues became part of the Jewish religious scene, people gathered in them on the sabbath for worship and study of the Scriptures. The New Testament indicates the first Christians were Jews, many of whom continued to worship in the Temple and meet in synagogues. As Christians became more aware of other distinctiveness, they met in homes for fellowship, worship, and study. Later they began to congregate in special buildings—churches. Still, the family remained the center of worship and religious instruction.

Worship practices in churches have changed greatly through the centuries, but worship by families has remained much the same. Informal family worship usually includes reading the Bible, praying, expressing needs, remembering absent members, and singing. Sometimes family worship is more formal with candles, devotionals, and special music. Whether formal or informal, the event centers in expressing the "worthship" of God for the devotion of the entire family.

Worship means just that—worthship, that God is worth everything we are and have. Worship is expressed by how a family uses its talents and possessions. If we spend more for personal luxuries than for extending the gospel, the message is clear: we care more about things than we do about God. If more is spent on play and frivolous items than on sending missionaries around the world to preach the gospel, our talk about how much we love God comes through to others as shallow and hypocritical. Worship is expressed in daily family life by relating to one another in Christian love, by being fair and thoughtful, by showing that God is alive and well in family routine. Worship ought never be a dull, boring experience. Rather it is to be a discovery of how wonderful God is. Worship is sharing the miracles which God performs in life, the prayers that he answers, the joy that he gives.

Has your family disciplined itself for a regular time of worship? Do you have a certain place for worship? What plan do you use? Do you vary the procedure to avoid the dullness of routine? Is worship a show parents put on for children or do adults maintain worship when children are not present? How do you utilize the Bible in worship? Other devotional material? What contribution does each family member make? How do you overcome the problem of busyness, fractured family life, and conflicting time schedules? Family worship calls for careful planning, dedication, and effort—but it's worth it.

IV.

Finally, *discipleship is expressed in family life through ministry and service.* The people of Israel, as they moved into the Promised Land, were given special commandments about care for strangers, the poor, orphans, and widows. Each family unit was primarily responsible for seeing that its members did not suffer want and that strangers who came through the land were cared for.

In the New Testament the emphasis on care for the poor and powerless by the family continued. Jesus taught that children were responsible for aging parents. Church leaders declared that a person who did not provide for his own family was worse than an infidel. Christian families were urged to share what they possessed with persons in need. Babies were rescued from garbage heaps where they had been dumped by pagan Romans to die or to be snatched by brothel owners who would raise them for prostitution or sell them into slavery. Widows were placed on special rolls to be supported by Christian families.

Such display of ministry and service did not go unnoticed in the pagan world. Pagans began to say about these Christian families, "There is something different about them. They care about one another. They are cohesive, but more than that they reach out to touch others in love and ministry." The non-Christians also noticed that the families of believers stood against practices which tended to destroy human life. They attacked social issues which reeked with injustice. In a sexually polluted society they took their stand for purity. In a world where slavery was cruel they dared declare that slaves were to be treated as brothers and sisters in Christ. They tore down walls which separated people into hostile camps. These families demonstrated that they were different.

A ministering kind of family life is expressed today by many Christians. Is it expressed in your family? What have you done recently for someone outside your family? Whom have you gone to see, called on, written, taken gifts to, shared job opportunities with, brought in to the fellowship when they were lonely and frightened? Have you helped the separated, divorced, and widowed feel the warmth of your own family setting?

The discipleship of the people of God is expressed in our families through Christian nurture, evangelism, worship, and ministry. I wonder if I've described your family? If I haven't, would you talk to God about helping you to make it conform to his way? And will you pray for others that each family of Christians will be truly a family of God?

13
Expressing Discipleship in the World

Romans 12:1-2; 3:1-7; Colossians 3:22 to 4:1

Christian discipleship is never a purely personal matter. It involves all we are as well as all of our relationships. It affects all of the institutions and orders of human society—not only churches but also schools, governments, labor unions, businesses, and recreation functions. Three dimensions of discipleship in the world are highlighted by the New Testament: work, recreation, and citizenship. All three are means by which we can express our faith in God and demonstrate discipleship.

I.

Discipleship is to be expressed through our daily work. The third chapter of Colossians includes instructions on the economic aspect of discipleship. Remember that the economy of the first century was basically a slave-master operation rather than our employer-employee relation. The text declares: "Slaves, obey your human masters in all things, and do it not only when they are watching you, just to gain their approval, but do it with a sincere heart, because of your reverence for the Lord. Whatever you do, work at it with all your heart, as though you were working for the Lord, and not for men. Remember that the Lord will reward you; you will receive what he has kept for his people. For Christ is the real Master you serve. And the wrongdoer, whoever he is, will be paid for the wrong things he does; for God judges everyone by the same standard. Masters, be right and fair in the way you treat your slaves. Remember that you too have a Master in heaven" (Col. 3:22 to 4:1, TEV).

God created us to live according to a work-rest, labor-play cycle. Work six days, the Commandment says, and rest on the seventh. Work is part of life. Mankind was created to work just as the birds were created to fly. Paul commanded the early Christians to not steal but work honestly. He instructed the Thessalonian Christians not to feed their fellow believers who were too busy being religious to work and earn their own food. Idleness is condemned in the Bible and industry is praised. A healthy but lazy Christian who does not work diligently is an inadequate disciple. The believer who earns his own living, on the other hand, can be an effective witness. "In this way you will win the respect of those who are not believers, and will not have to depend on anyone for what you need" (1 Thess. 4:12, TEV).

Specific instruction about daily work is given in Colossians. Paul indicates that a Christian will do his daily work well. Workers are divided into two categories, those who work for others and those for whom others work. Those who work for others are to do it diligently and honestly, realizing that they are actually working for God, not for another human being. They are to be God-pleasers, not men-pleasers. Work is done as service to God— whether it is driving a truck, performing surgery, teaching elementary school students, farming, or ranching. All useful work can be God-pleasing—mind and muscle work, blue-collar and white-collar jobs, inside and outdoor labor, employee and employer posts. At the end of every day a person ought to be able to say, "I did it for you, heavenly Father. I place what I did in your hands and trust that you can use it."

The Bible also indicates that those who are employers, supervisors, owners, and managers have a responsibility. They are to treat those who work for them equitably and well, to pay wages which are fair, to see that people have job conditions which are decent, to see that everyone has a fair opportunity to display talent and ability. They are to provide guidance, motivation, and incentive. As Paul put it, "Remember that you too have a Master in heaven."

Many in the world of work separate what they do on the job from what they do in their church. Daily work activities seem to have no relation to Sunday worship, Wednesday prayer meeting, or other church activities. Faithful in church, they are unfaithful to God's standards of honesty, integrity, and righteousness in daily work. Others feel if they don't curse on the job, steal from their employer, or do something starkly immoral, God is satisfied with their work. The Bible says more is required. The disciple works for God and so performs his job as unto the Lord. He does his best. Even if his supervisor doesn't notice the good job and reward him, the disciple keeps doing his best because ultimately he's working for God who knows everything and rewards those who work well. Paul wrote to the Ephesians, "Do your work as slaves cheerfully, then, as though you served the Lord, and not merely men. Remember that the Lord will reward every man, whether slave or free, for the good work he does" (6:7-8, TEV).

The principle of Christian discipleship at work applies to every type of labor. Take school, for example. The student's work world is school. A person who is capable of doing academic work well but does it sloppily is showing poor discipleship. God doesn't expect everybody to make A's, but he expects everyone to do his best. God doesn't expect everyone to be an honor student, but he expects everyone to do each task as unto God. If you are writing a term paper for Mrs. A. or Mr. X., you may have a tendency to do it just to please the teacher, or perhaps for a good grade. If you write the paper for God, you will want to do it in a far better way. Similarly, teachers who are Christians will teach not to please students, principals, parents, or school board members, but God. The Christian teacher will do the best job possible regardless of the time, energy, or effort required.

As you look back over the past week in the world of work—school, business, profession, home, labor, or whatever—did you really labor for God? Are you satisfied with the quality of your work and with the way you treated people with whom you worked? We'll never make the impact God wants us to make on our world until we have become disciples in every dimension of life, including the economic. Think what it would mean if every Christian in your town expressed discipleship in daily work.

II.

Christian discipleship can be expressed in leisure and recreation as well as daily work. What is to be the Christian's basic stance in the world? In the book of Romans, Paul spent eleven chapters laying a theological foundation on which he erected an ethical superstructure, a description of the Christian life in relation to the world. Romans 12 begins with a call to discipleship related to recreation and leisure. "So then, my brothers, because of God's great mercy to us, I make this appeal to you: Offer yourselves as a living sacrifice to God, dedicated to his service and pleasing to him. This is the true worship that you should offer. Do not conform outwardly to the standards of this world, but let God transform you inwardly by a complete change of your mind. Then you will be able to know the will of God—what is good, and is pleasing to him, and is perfect" (vv. 1-2, TEV).

In essence, the Bible says, "Don't let the world cram you into its mold. Instead, do what God wants you to do and you will mold the world. You set the standards. Don't let the standards of the world determine your action."

Many people find it difficult in the world of leisure and recreation to maintain Christian standards. Pressures to conform to the world's standards come from every side and in many packages—movies, television programs, popular songs, drugs, gambling, alcohol, pornography, and many others. In each the appeal is to pleasure, often in a way degrading to human life and to God. People taunt, "Come on. Do it! What's the matter? Are you a religious fanatic or something? Don't be a straight arrow. Have some fun. Enjoy life. You only go around once."

The implication is that God doesn't want anyone to have fun, that he is a killjoy. That is a lie! Whenever you are determining what you're going to do for fun, recreation, and leisure, remember God wants you to have a good time. His desire for you is a rich, rewarding, joyful life. God's "don'ts" are directed to us for our own good. God made us and knows what will bring us true happiness. So he puts up roadsigns along our way because he loves us: "Warning! Danger Ahead! Go slow! Stop!"

If you'll follow God's will, let his mind rule your thoughts, allow his ways to become your ways, you will find genuine happiness. After all, who are you going to trust? Someone who will profit from your "fun?" A fairweather friend? Or your heavenly Father who loves you so much he sent his Son to be your Savior?

Some people disobey God's will in refusing to recreate. They are what some term "workaholics." Feeling they must work all the time, they suffer pangs of guilt when not on the job. A craving for things, praise, or achievement drives some to ceaseless labor. Others are restless, suffering from excessively high energy levels. Some betray a lack of faith in God; ignoring the commandment to rest one day in seven, they work all of the time as if such frantic effort could gain them security. Rest and relaxation are necessary if we are to follow God's will.

What kind of leisure life does God will for us, though? That's a big question. Since our society affords more leisure time for more people than any other in history, it is an especially important issue. Recreation is a problem for many young people because of the pressures they encounter from parents, society, and other youth. Parents who want their offspring to be popular at any price push them into social activities which are potentially dangerous. Society sets a steady series of temptation traps ranging from advertisements to books and articles describing what the "in" thing for fun is this year.

Peer pressure is intense; generally youth want more than anything to please their peers, to be accepted by the popular group. Conversations often run like this: "What are you going to do tonight?" "Oh, I don't know. What are you going to do tonight?" "Oh, I don't know. What are you going to do tonight?" Finally somebody sets a course, lifts a standard, moves in a particular direction and others begin to fall in behind the leader. At that point it's hard to say no. Courage coupled with strong Christian convictions are called for.

Coping with leisure-time pressure is also difficult for many adults. They face temptations too. Sure they have the advantage of experience which ought to help them know what is right, but unfortunately many adults are slow learners regarding morality and leisure. Adults face another pressure: to use recreation as part of their work. In trying to close a business deal, it's tempting to do what you think will please clients, what will give them pleasure and therefore make them more willing to do business. The Bible says the Christian is not to lose control of life to anyone other than God. We've got to set God's standards in our own lives and not let the world cram us into its mold.

Discipleship is expressed by how we play as well as by how we pray. How we recreate demonstrates at least as much about our relation to God as how we worship. What we do in our leisure may be a more potent witness than what we do in church. I trust your discipleship in leisure is being expressed in such a way that God can say, "Well done. I like what you are doing." If that's the case, you are finding fulfillment and real joy.

III.

A third way discipleship is expressed in the world is through citizenship and politics. Some people don't believe the Christian faith has anything to do with politics. Many parents don't want their offspring to go into politics. A recent poll taken among church members revealed that only a minority would be happy if their sons or daughters went into politics. The majority indicated that they felt politics was dirty business and they feared their offspring would be contaminated if they got involved. They implied that people who had any sense of self-respect wouldn't get into politics and certainly wouldn't run for public office.

The Bible views government, politics, and citizenship in a more positive way. In the Old Testament the political leaders were quite often the religious leaders. Many Old Testament heroes we hold in high esteem, those we urge people to pattern their life after, were political activists and government leaders. Moses, Joshua, Samuel, David, and Isaiah, for example, were all political figures.

In the New Testament the circumstances are different. The Roman government had conquered Israel and there was no longer any government in Israel except Roman governors or puppet rulers under Rome. No religious leaders, therefore, emerged as political leaders. In such a setting you'd expect silence in the Word of

God on government or instructions to resist the atheistic power of Rome. To the contrary, several passages relate to government and you find clear instructions to the Christians to be responsible to their rulers. I personally think it's very interesting that in the book of Romans you find the clearest instructions about government; this book was written to the heart of the Roman Empire. In fact, some of the people who first read the book of Romans, which stresses obedience to government authorities, were in Caesar's household.

Here is what Paul wrote in the thirteenth chapter of Romans about the political dimension of discipleship: "Everyone must obey the state authorities, because no authority exists without God's permission, and the existing authorities have been put there by God. Whoever opposes the existing authority opposes what God has ordered; and anyone who does so will bring judgment on himself. For rulers are not to be feared by those who do good but by those who do evil. Would you like to be unafraid of the man in authority? Then do what is good, and he will praise you. For he is God's servant working for your own good. But if you do evil, be afraid of him, for his power to punish is real. He is God's servant and carries out God's wrath on those who do evil. For this reason you must obey the authorities—not just because of God's wrath, but also as a matter of conscience. This is also the reason that you pay taxes, for the authorities are working for God when they fulfill their duties. Pay, then, what you owe them: pay them your personal and property taxes, and show respect and honor for them all" (vv. 1-7, TEV).

The major portion of the New Testament has a political tone to it. Why? Why all this talk about rendering to Caesar, paying taxes, obeying the powers that be, praying for the emperor, and the like? Keep in mind that Jesus was crucified in the eyes of the world as a political revolutionary. He was labeled an insurrectionist, a troublemaker trying to undermine the Roman state. As the word about the Christian movement spread throughout the Empire, Romans often thought of Christians as being subversives, revolutionaries, and seditionists.

The word spread about the early Christians was, "You'd better watch them. You can't trust them. They are unpatriotic." Therefore, much of the writing of the Christian community attempted to counter these rumors by showing that Jesus operated within the laws of the state and so did his followers. The book of Romans points out that although Jesus was executed on a Roman cross as a revolutionary, the real reason he died was for the sins of the world—including the sins of the Romans who killed him. Further, those who trust Jesus are enjoined to be model citizens, thus laying in the grave the rumor that Christians were unpatriotic at best and traitors at worst.

If you take the Bible seriously, therefore, you must take citizenship seriously. You can't be a good Christian if you are not a good citizen. The bad citizenship of good people is partly responsible for bringing our nation to the condition it's in today. There is no outline in the New Testament about Christian political activities. In those first days of the faith, a Christian did not run *for* the Roman Senate; he ran *from* the Roman Senate. Furthermore, specific instructions to persons living in the first century under Roman dictatorship would hardly be applicable to twentieth-century Americans living in a democracy.

Nevertheless, the New Testament gives clear direction to Christians concerning political responsibility. The thirteenth chapter of Romans is an example. Christians are to pay taxes and obey rulers, being careful that their citizenship stance causes no derogatory comment to be made by the world. Obedience and taxation linked with prayer were the first-century Christian's basic means of seeing that government functioned well.

Today, in a democracy, the Christian's responsibility for government includes other measures—voting, volunteering for civic tasks, aiding in elections, and running for office. We need disciplined Christians who take their stand in government—at the conference tables of city councils, in the courthouses of county government, in the state capitals of our various states, and in the Federal Government throughout the nation. If God moves you in that direction, don't dig your heels in and protest that politics is dirty business. Follow God's direction to minister through government. Every vocation calls for some degree of dealing with unregenerate people, with accommodation, with efforts to work out the best possible solution in the midst of differing ideas.

Disciples are not an extinct variety of Homo sapiens who wore bathrobes and sandals following a carpenter named Jesus through Roman provinces centuries ago. Disciples are alive and well today. We still follow Jesus, committed to his way, but in the trappings of the twentieth century.

We're discovering that discipleship is a lifelong adventure involving faith, growth, joy, and sometimes hurt. Like salt, it changes the flavor of every dimension of life—witness, church, family, work, leisure, and politics. And like salt that is no longer effective, life without discipleship is flat, tasteless, and useless. "Come, follow me," Jesus said. Yes, do that, and express your discipleship in all of life.

Notes

1.
Life Under the Cross

1. *Jesus Christ and His Cross* (Philadelphia: Westminster Press, 1953), p. 139.
2. *Evangelistic Sermons* (Nashville: Broadman Press, 1953), p. 104.
3. *The Cross in Christian Experience* (New York: George H. Doran Co., 1908), pp. 233-36.
4. *The Cost of Discipleship* (New York: The Macmillan Company, 1959), pp. 79-81.
5. *Stains on Glass Windows* (Waco: Word Books, 1969), p. 5.
6. *The Imitation of Christ* (New York: Grosset & Dunlap, nd), p. 106.

2.
Discipleship: Impulsive or Reflective?

1. Eugenia Price, *Early Will I Seek Thee* (Westwood, N.J.: Fleming H. Revell Company, 1956), pp. 131-41.
2. Ralph S. Cushman, *The Message of Stewardship* (Nashville: Abingdon-Cokesbury Press, 1946), pp. 210-11.

3.
The Disciple's Witness

1. Quoted in Dale Moody, *The Hope of Glory* (Grand Rapids: Wm. B. Eerdmans Publishing Co., 1964), p. 13.
2. "The Pulley," in Mark Van Doren, *An Anthology of World Poetry* (New York: Harcourt Brace & Co., 1936), p. 1086.

3. Moody, *op. cit.*, p. 33.

4. *Christian Reflections* (Grand Rapids: Wm. B. Eerdmans Publishing Co., 1967), p. 173.

5. *The Mystery of Being*, Pt. II, Gateway Edition (Chicago: Henry Regnery Co., 1960), p. 149.

4.
Disciples in the Making

1. From *The New International Version New Testament*. Copyright © 1973, The New York Bible Society International. Used by permission.

2. *The Ethic of Jesus in the Teaching of the Church* (Nashville: Abingdon Press, 1961), pp. 7,40 ff.

3. "Matthew," *Interpreter's Bible* (Nashville: Abingdon-Cokesbury, 1951), vol. VIII, p. 622.

4. *Out of the Depths* (Grand Rapids: Wm. B. Eerdmans Publishing Co., 1962), p. 67.

5. *Commentary on Luke* (Waco: Word Books, 1972), p. 338.

6. *Ethics and the Gospels* (New York: Charles Scribner's Sons, 1960), p. 68.

6.
Discipleship as Discipline

1. C. Roy Angell, *Baskets of Silver* (Nashville: Broadman Press, 1955), pp. 38-40.

7.
Discipleship and the Devotional Life

1. E. Glenn Hinson, *A Serious Call to a Contemplative Lifestyle* (Philadelphia: The Westminster Press, 1974).

The Authors

Nolan P. Howington is curriculum consultant, Church Training Department, Baptist Sunday School Board, Nashville. Before coming to this position, he was pastor of churches in Knoxville and Little Rock and taught Christian ethics at Southern Baptist Seminary for ten years. A native of Georgia, Dr. Howington is a graduate of Wake Forest University (B.A., M.A.) and Southern Baptist Seminary (Th.M., Ph.D.) with graduate study at the University of Edinburgh. He has been active in denominational and community life and is a popular preacher and conference leader.

Alton H. McEachern is pastor, First Baptist Church, Greensboro, North Carolina, the largest congregation in the state. Previously he served churches in Kentucky, West Virginia, Indiana, and Georgia. Both Southern Baptist and Midwestern Baptist seminaries have invited him to teach special courses in preaching. His education was based in his native Georgia at Truett-McConnell College and Mercer University (B.A.); his theological studies were completed at Southern Baptist Seminary (M.Div., Th.M., D.Min.) with graduate work at Glasgow, Oxford, and Princeton. His book *Proclaim the Gospel* was published in 1975 by Convention Press.

William M. Pinson, Jr. is pastor, First Baptist Church, Wichita Falls, Texas, one of the larger churches in that state. For fifteen years he had taught Christian ethics at Southwestern Baptist Seminary; he had also worked with the Christian Life Commission of Texas Baptists. Dr. Pinson is a native of Texas and a graduate of North Texas State University (B.A.) and Southwestern Baptist Seminary (B.D., Th.D., M.Div.). His graduate study has been at the University of Edinburgh and Texas Christian University. He has been active in denominational life and has written four books and collaborated on three other works.